Holy Ground

Holy Ground

CELTIC CHRISTIAN SPIRITUALITY

Deborah K. Cronin

UPPER
ROOM BOOKS
NASHVILLE

HOLY GROUND:
CELTIC CHRISTIAN SPIRITUALITY
© 1999 by Deborah K. Cronin
All rights reserved.

Art Direction and Cover Design: Harriette Bateman
Cover Photograph: The cover photograph is a reproduction of the Symbols of the Four Evangelists found on Folio 27V in *The Book of Kells.* It is used by permission of The Board of Trinity College Dublin.
Interior Design: Harriette Bateman
Interior Illustrations: Cari Buziak <www.cadvision.com/attoboy/cari>

The Upper Room Web Site: http://www.upperroom.org
First printing: 1999

Library of Congress Cataloging-in-Publication Data

Cronin, Deborah K.
    Holy ground : Celtic Christian spirituality / by Deborah K. Cronin.
        p.   cm.
    Includes bibliographical references.
    ISBN 0-8358-0838-6
    1. Rural clergy—Religious life. 2. Spirituality—Celtic Church.
I. Title.
BV638.7.C76   1999
253'.09173'4—dc21   98-37058

Printed in the United States of America

To the congregations and pastors of the Mountain View District

of The United Methodist Church

and

To Klaus, my late schnauzer

(He taught me to watch birds, chipmunks, and rabbits.)

CONTENTS

ACKNOWLEDGMENTS

$\mathcal{I}$ am blessed with a rich community of folks who encourage my writing and are patient with me when I engage in that task. Sandy Ahlgren has proofread several projects, including this one. Her patience and diligence are a blessing. Sandy Lasher, a lover of Celtic Christian art, encouraged and celebrated my progress in writing. A rural ministry class from United Theological Seminary at Buffalo endured my reading one chapter at the beginning of each class. Their enthusiasm for the project and feedback were most helpful. Myrtle Felkner was another cheerleader and helped out with reading a draft of the manuscript. Other readers included Paul Bigler, Linda Dolby, and Brian McGaffigan, who each made insightful comments. My secretary, Cheryl Isaman, suffered through it all and operated the fax machine as we gathered permissions to use quotations. Her gracious and helpful assistance is always appreciated.

Two special groups of people contributed mightily to reading the manuscript. Bishop Rueben P. Job and John S. Mogabgab were recruited by The Upper Room to offer their critical comments. Their professional expertise was most appreciated. A group of laywomen, including Glenora Crowell, Sally Demming, Donna Hall, Louise Howe, and Lucy Stauring provided wonderful feedback from their perspective as teachers, librarians, and lovers of good Christian literature.

Carl Schultz, a professor of Old Testament at Houghton College, offered helpful biblical and theological insights. His gracious input was much appreciated.

My fellow superintendents (Dave Lubba, Larry Lundgren, Roy Miller, and Greg VanDussen) offered emotional support for the project, as did Bishop Hae-Jong Kim. I am grateful for the strong collegial relationship we share which undergirds all my work. As always, my mother Alice watched the project with both concern and interest and tolerated more than one vacation accompanied by the computer and my files on Celtic Christianity.

JoAnn Miller, Executive Editor for Upper Room Books, initially recognized the validity of the project. She later spoke just the right word of encouragement when I feared my work was not of the quality desired.

Finally, Janice Grana, Executive Editor for Upper Room Books, gave this project new life when I had just about given up. Her guidance was honest, gracious, and enabling. I am deeply appreciative for her assistance and enthusiasm.

PREFACE

*M*y encounter with Celtic Christianity has been a journey to islands.

I first journeyed to Ireland for Celtic Christian studies at Trinity College in Dublin. The following summer I made a pilgrimage to Scotland and the islands of Iona and Staffa. That same summer my Celtic Christian sojourn took me to my summer home. It is not an island in the geographical sense, but a retreat in the woods beside a quiet stream, an island in the midst of the busyness and stress of my work and ministry. There I dwelt richly with Celtic Christian poetry and prayers. I wrote most of the final draft of this manuscript on Jekyll Island, off the coast of Georgia and just south of St. Simon's Island, where the Wesleys encountered their ill-fated New World mission. My schnauzer, Klaus, faithfully plodded miles beside me on this island as we harvested a treasure in sand dollars and as the book's final form took shape in my mind and heart.

On Jekyll Island one morning at breakfast a man said to me, "We come to islands for peace." His observation, made in the midst of a discussion about various travel destinations, struck me as astutely spiritual. Islands are unique places, holy ground separated by water from other larger landmasses and surrounded by beaches, rocky shores, and cliffs where the light plays on the water, often producing revelations of sight and sound. Islands are places of vision. John "was on the island called Patmos because of the word of God and the testimony of Jesus" (Rev. 1:9) when a vision of heaven was revealed to him.

The islands of my Celtic Christian journey have been places where my heart has earnestly sung the ancient Irish hymn, "Be Thou my vision, O Lord of my heart; Naught be all else to me, save that Thou art." On these islands I found a renewed vision of God as Creator, Redeemer, and Holy Wind dancing in the sunlight on the beach and pounding in the crest of the waves.

Early Celtic Christianity, for the Irish Celts, was always a bit on the edge. The Romans never made it to Ireland, leaving the green isle just beyond the control of both the emperor and the pope. Thus this island birthed a Christian experience somewhat removed both geographically and theologically from mainland Europe. Patrick, evangelizing Ireland in the late fourth and early fifth centuries, probably never heard of Augustine of Hippo. Augustine blessed us in the early fifth century with a clearly stated formula of God's gift of unmerited grace, yet he was sadly bereft of the Celtic Christian notion of God's creation being a very good thing. And so Patrick quite cheerfully went about Ireland, seeding the gospel as he traveled, and celebrating the goodness of creation and humans in two kinds. Under the influence of Patrick's ministry, Ireland was converted to Christianity without the sacrifice of any martyrs. And, remarkably, before Patrick's death, the practice of both slavery and pagan human sacrifice had been eliminated from the verdant isle. Unlike the *Pax Romana*, which was based on the sword-in-hand Roman Empire, Patrick's *Pax Patricus* had a pronounced peace dividend.

While Celtic Christianity was found in Brittany (present-day northwestern France), it particularly flourished on several islands. Among these are the island including England, Wales, and Scotland; Ireland; Scotland's small but wondrous island of Iona; the isle of Skye; and Lindisfarne, a small island off the Northumbrian coast, connected to it at low tide by a causeway. We can only speculate about the reasons Celtic Christianity flourished on islands. Perhaps it was because Celtic Christianity has always been just a bit different from the mainstream. It is Christianity mingled with, but not compromised by, the finest aspects of pagan Celtism, those that found resonance with Christian symbols and understandings. Celtic Christianity was never overly concerned with ecclesiastical matters, preferring to find its way among and with everyday people (including women!). Its earliest adherents were persons of great creativity and whimsy who learned to spin the Gospels into golden storytelling events and who dedicated themselves to illustrating those same stories with playful, yet extraordinarily beautiful, pen-and-ink artistry. Celtic Christianity is also the story of highly effective and revered holy leaders such as Patrick (390–461 C.E.), Brigid (452–524 C.E.), and Columba (521–597 C.E.), each appearing in his or her own island of time.

The golden age of Celtic Christianity was itself an island in time, an all-too-brief moment between the fifth and eleventh centuries. During this time Europe was shrouded by the Dark Ages (476–1000 C.E.) and languished under pagan control and domination. Isolated and cutoff from Roman influence, Celtic Christianity first flourished by itself and then struggled on mightily in the face of Viking invaders during the late eighth century through the eleventh century. The so-called rediscovery of Celtic Christianity in the late twentieth century has been like finding a lost island, one rich in treasure buried long ago not by pirates, but by those faithful ones who valued it as a pearl of great worth.

My own spiritual journey with Celtic Christianity has provided me with an island vision in the midst of challenging ministry. When I became a United Methodist district superintendent four years ago, I recognized more than ever before that I needed to focus on my own spiritual formation. I needed to look at who I am and why I believe as I do. I needed to examine some of the ghosts of my family's religious experience, particularly those of my father, a spiritual man who regrettably was not a

Christian. I needed a means by which to nurture my own soul, often challenged by the stress and responsibility of my work. I knew I needed to pray as I had never prayed before, and that I needed to pray in a new way that would bring revival to my heart and mind. I also knew that I needed to offer a vision for spiritual formation to the pastors and congregations I was called to superintend.

I have a hunch that many people, like myself, find themselves stepping back to take spiritual inventory when faced with a life or job transition. Perhaps you have done this or are even now in the midst of this type of appraisal. During times of change and transition, pressures and tensions can intensify and seem overburdening. Also, change does not usually impact just one area of our lives. For example, a job change can impact our relationships with family and friends. The last child leaving home upsets the household routine and expectations. A parent grown frail and ill places new demands on our already busy lives. These experiences press upon our minds and hearts with double weight and hardship. It is easy to lose your sense of self in the midst of them, thus forgetting to take care of your own body, mind, and heart.

During these stressful times our spiritual vision and commitment may grow dim. It is important to seek spiritual self-care—experiences of island retreat during times such as these. My hope is that encountering Celtic Christianity will be like an island retreat for you. Find a quiet place for your reading, perhaps in the woods or in a desert rock garden. The important thing is to seek a place where, even for a few hours, you can be alone in the presence of God. In such a place you may find yourself more able to pray in the tradition of Celtic Christians: with awareness of the full blessing of the Trinity, with deep appreciation for God's creation, and with a renewed sense of your relationship to humanity.

As you take note of God's creation surrounding you, I hope God will speak to you through the stories of Celtic Christians like Patrick, Columba, and Brigid. Their stories offer new ways to celebrate God's ability to work through history and people to bring peace and wholeness to humanity. Even more, I hope you will hear God's voice speaking through your own faith stories. Savor these stories as you recall them. Let them roll around in your mind and heart. Live into them once again as you recall how they impact your life. Allow yourself to recall and intertwine your stories into the experience of Celtic Christian spirituality. As you seek and find the spiritual island where you are able to recall the stories of your own faith, you may discover renewed vision for your spiritual journey.

For Celtic Christians, vision is not something elusive or ephemeral. Neither is it vague, humdrum, or mundane. Rather, the Celtic Christian understanding of vision is real, tangible, and of God. It is also a bit on the wild side. It reminds me of the extraordinary sight I witnessed one night in a community dance garden in

Killarney. There I watched several generations of one Irish family dance the night away in what could only be described as a combination of Irish stepdancing (now made famous with the dance concert phenomenon, *Riverdance*) and the exhausting Italian tarantella. Their feet flew, they never stopped smiling and shouting for joy, and the look on their faces was one of radiant transport and blessing. Watching them left me breathless, exuberant, and rejuvenated.

Watching them also reminded me that who we are, what we believe, and what brings both joy and sorrow to our hearts are often determined by our family relationships. As you will see, the *tuath*, or tribal, relationships were part of what defined the Celtic Christian experience. Likewise, the family experiences we inherit often define our spiritual vision. Examining the boundaries of this vision can help us to understand where we need to stretch and reshape our own spiritual presuppositions and understandings.

Today, we too often think of the Christian experience of vision as simply a step in goal setting. Attaining vision can become simply a process in church or even personal decision making, some tool we need, so that we can arrive where we think we already want to go. For Celtic Christians the experience of vision is one of seeing what God has done and then seeing it through God's creative eyes, followed by seeing the life-giving possibilities God sees. The vision may take actual shape in the viewer's eye, or it may simply be a vision of the heart and mind that leaves one breathless and numb.

We sing the words to "Be Thou My Vision" lightly, because they are familiar to us. Celtic Christians, however, most often surrounded by both water and the Divinity, sing the traditional words of this Celtic Christian hymn from the deep recesses of the heart:

> Be Thou my vision, O Lord of my heart;
> Naught be all else to me save that Thou art,
> Thou my best thought, by day or by night,
> Waking and sleeping, Thy presence my light.
>
> Be Thou my wisdom, be Thou my true word;
> I ever with Thee, and Thou with me, Lord;
> Thou my great Father, I Thy true son;
> Thou in me dwelling, and I with Thee one.
>
> Be Thou my breastplate, my sword for the fight;
> Be Thou my armor, and be Thou my might;
> Thou my soul's shelter, Thou my high tower;
> Raise Thou me heavenward, O power of my power.
>
> Riches I heed not, nor man's empty praise;
> Thou my inheritance, now and always;
> Thou and Thou only, first in my heart,
> High King of heaven, my treasure Thou art.

High King of heaven, my victory won,
May I reach heaven's joys, O bright heaven's sun!
Heart of my heart, whatever befall,
Still be my vision, O ruler of all.

Eighth-century Irish Hymn
Translated Mary Byrne (1880–1931)
Versified Eleanor Hull (1860–1935)

The light of heaven that no darkness can extinguish shines through the verses of this hymn. The wisdom of God's Word, which readily captured Celtic hearts in the fifth through eleventh centuries, is celebrated for its indwelling presence. The protection afforded by God finds concrete expression in references to armor, echoing the apostle Paul's words as found in Ephesians 6:11: "Put on the whole armor of God." God is compared to a strong tower like the towers the Celtic Christian monks built so they could hide their precious hand-copied manuscripts of the Gospels from Viking invaders and save themselves from slaughter. The hymn sings of God as being the High King of heaven. In our own day, we may shy away from these words, seeing them as not being politically correct, but this reference tells us that Celtic Christians in Ireland claimed a vision of God as being more powerful than Ireland's seemingly omnipotent high kings. This hymn, unfortunately translated in many newer hymnals so as to render it devoid of its rich Celtic Christian symbols, aptly summarizes much of what it means to embrace the Celtic Christian vision of the Christian faith.

"Be Thou My Vision" echoes the sentiment found in The Revelation to John in which John describes being on the island called Patmos and "in the spirit on the Lord's day" (Rev. 1:10). What John heard and saw on that island was pure vision, the vision of Jesus the Christ, crucified, risen, and glorified. My Celtic Christian journeys to islands have brought me a renewed sense of this pure vision. My prayer is that you, too, in your encounter with Celtic Christian spirituality, will discover your heart and mind surrounded by the waters of your baptism and the light of the crucified and risen Christ.

*F*or the beauty of the earth, for the glory of the skies,
  for the love which from our birth over and around us lies, . . .

For the beauty of each hour of the day and of the night,
  hill and vale, and tree and flower,
  sun and moon, and stars of light;

Lord of all, to thee we raise this our hymn of grateful praise.

—*Folliot S. Pierpoint*

CHAPTER 1

ALL THE EARTH IS SACRED

I write these words on Iona, a wild, windy, yet holy island off the rugged west coast of Scotland. This place is as remote as you will find in Western Europe. Sturdy Percheron horses pull small carts here. Few cars travel upon Iona's tiny one-lane roads. Sheep graze everywhere. Their plaintive cries are heard throughout the day and night. Birds, especially seagulls and puffins, fly against the wind, landing wherever the wind currents will allow. A few folks make a living fishing and a few more raise sheep and lambs. Another handful ekes out a meager seasonal income from the pilgrims who make the long journey to Iona, located in the North Atlantic's Inner Hebrides Islands. This place is simple, harsh, and daunting. And yet, this place—this very remote place—is holy ground.

Something happened on Iona fourteen centuries ago, in 562 C.E., which proved to Christendom that the message of Christ could make seemingly insignificant places truly great. A man named Columba sailed from his Irish homeland in a tiny curragh, a frail, open, leather boat, to this small island. The reason he came is not clear. The well-known legend is that he was born to Christian parents, became a deacon, and eventually founded a church and monastery in Derry. Columba encountered a copy of *St. Martin's Psalter* that belonged to Finnian of Molville. Columba loved the psalter and, because he desired it strongly, hand copied the manuscript in secret. This infuriated Finnian. Columba was brought before the Irish high king, Diarmait. Diarmait rendered a judgment against Columba and forced him to surrender the copied psaltér to Finnian, decreeing, "To every cow her calf; to every book its copy." Interestingly, this is thought to be the first copyright case in history.

Columba went home and, being a tribal chieftain's son, raised a small army of his kin that he led in battle against Diarmait. The battle left three thousand of Diarmait's soldiers dead. Only one of Columba's soldiers died, this attributed to a miracle on Columba's behalf. Almost excommunicated for the deed, Columba was instead exiled from Ireland and sent to a cold, windy, and damp island off the west coast of Scotland (then known as Pictland). As an added punishment, this island was just far enough from Ireland that Columba could not see his beloved homeland. Here he founded a monastery. It

became Iona, a famous center for Celtic Christian spiritual growth and study. Columba is reported to have replied to one of his monks who commented on the island, saying, "This place is so small," with these words: "Yes, but someday it will be great."

This is the stuff of legends. Another version of Columba's story recalls that he, the son of an Irish king, became a Christian priest. He then came to Iona simply for the purpose of building a cultural, business, and religious stronghold for his clan, which was establishing a colonial beachhead on the western coast of Scotland. Regardless of which story you believe, Iona did become a great place from which Christianity was introduced into Scotland and where many volumes of the scriptures were painstakingly copied by hand and illuminated with wondrous paintings.

Columba knew, despite his fellow monk's misgivings, that when he arrived on Iona he was standing on holy ground. Isolated, small, primitive, seemingly desolate Iona was sacred land to Columba because he trusted that on this island God would do mystical and magnificent things. He also knew and trusted that God, whose love will not let any of us go, would love him in this isolated place.

Celtic Christian spirituality can help you embrace the created world in which you live as God's special gift to you. Whether you live in an urban or rural setting, God is seeking to bless your faith and ministry through the holy ground upon which you exist. *Spirituality* is a word not found in the Bible. And yet, that is exactly what is being expressed here: Celtic Christian spirituality as a way of understanding that God, whose very Spirit, whose breath (*ruach*) is breathed into all of creation, blows through all places and all locations. Jesus said: "The wind blows where it chooses, and you hear the sound of it, but you do not know where it comes from or where it goes. So it is with everyone who is born of the Spirit" (John 3:8). Whether your work and ministry take you down busy city streets or over country lanes, the breath of God, God's Holy Spirit, is there to bless you.

This book, in its completed form, is far different from the book I anticipated. Initially, I journeyed into Celtic Christianity in search of my Irish, Scottish, and English ancestral spiritual roots. What I discovered was the richness of Celtic Christianity, a richness grounded in deep faith in Christ, the power of the Trinity, and the simultaneous celebration of the Creator and creation. Because I am engaged in rural ministry I came to believe that Celtic Christianity is a gift to all who live in rural areas and are seeking to serve God as Christian disciples in these communities. But because of valued colleagues and friends who are not afraid to push me in my thoughts and reflections, I have come to appreciate how Celtic Christianity can inspire and support those who live in urban places. This appreciation grew when I visited the Iona Community, an ecumenical Celtic Christian community with many intercity lay and clergy members from Glasgow and other urban centers around the world.

Creation, the gift of the Creator, does not solely belong to outdoorsy people and those who live in meadows and forests. I love the last two chapters of Revelation, with their marvelous blending of both urban and rural images. I have found these images valuable when intertwined in my own thoughts and prayers. Our ultimate goal as Christians is to one day fellowship with God in an eternal city adorned with jewels from rural mines and quarries (jasper, sapphire, agate, emerald, onyx, carnelian, chrysolite, beryl, topaz, chrysoprase, jacinth, amethyst, pearl, and gold), a clean, crystal-bright river, and a tree bearing twelve kinds of fruit (Rev. 21:19–21; 22:1–2). This sacred mixture of urban and rural images is the holy ground of heaven, as described by John of Patmos.

This glorious picture of heaven, however, does not mitigate the unique setting of the rural world where God's creative handiwork is so readily apparent. Many, if not most, rural folks know that the ground upon which they live, breathe, love, and work is holy ground. These people, including farmers, ranchers, and miners, live close to the earth. Rural life for them is reflective of living in what the Celts called the "thin places." Heaven (and hell, for that matter) are only a blink of an eye away. For Celtic Christians there simply is little or no division between the natural world and the spiritual world. Their world is a "thin place," accommodating a tradition of imaginary faeries and leprechauns scampering between the various dimensions of existence and, far better still, with God very

near. The powerful presence of God's flora and fauna reminds them that they are living in the midst of things both seen and unseen. Another way to describe this is to speak of a "liminal place—where earth and heaven seem to meet and there is a sense that God is not far away."[1]

With no imagined separation between this reality and the reality of other places, it is possible for Celtic Christians to acknowledge all of creation, including even barnyard animals, as "very good" and worthy of God's loving attention. Thus we find this poetic expression:

> Come, Mary, and milk my cow,
> Come, Bride, and encompass her,
> Come, Columba the benign,
> And twine thine arms around my cow.
> Ho my heifer, ho my gentle heifer . . .
> My heifer dear, gentle and kind.
> For the sake of the High King, take to thy calf.[2]

If we step back from urban areas and view them from a wider perspective, we can see that they, too, are the gift of God's creative hand. Often when I visit a city, I try to imagine what it was like before the infrastructure was built. Where were the hills, the deep ravines and valleys?

Were they covered with woods, meadows, or desert? Focusing on those natural features I then, in my mind's eye, remove the buildings and streets. What then lies before me is a part of God's holy earth. I like to think that God created this place with its natural features such as river junctions and harbors so that people would congregate for commerce and communication. And out of this God-given natural gathering place the city arose, its infrastructure built by human hands created for this task. Thus I believe that God had a reason for creating this holy place. Its founding was not accidental, but was and still is special to the Creator.

Although Celtic Christianity sprang forth in a rural culture devoid of cities, it also birthed Ireland's first city. Brigid, the legendary Celtic Christian abbess, founded Kildare ("Church of the Oak") in 490 C.E. It quickly became a renowned monastic city-state located just southwest of present-day Dublin. Historical written records validating the life of Brigid are probably not reliable. However, we can assume she did exist since the community founded in her name thrived for centuries and because Celtic Christians rank her influence with that of Patrick and Columba, for whom we have authenticating documents.

Under Brigid's leadership Kildare became a metropolitan Christian community famous for its hospitality. It was well organized and orderly, providing safety for all people, including fugitives seeking sanctuary. Kildare was also a place where the hungry were fed and the sick and injured, healed. Its church was the largest in Ireland at that time. The monastic city-state of Kildare synthesized the finest aspects of both the Celtic and Christian cultures. This city was holy ground for all who found refuge within its walls.

Recently I visited an inner-city church. Being a person who is very comfortable in rural settings, my first response to this church and its neighborhood was to wonder why anyone would want to live there. My second response was to feel deep shame at my reaction. What I found inside the walls of that church was a multicultural congregation committed to ridding the neighborhood of drug houses, loneliness, poverty, and despair. This congregation and its pastors have learned to love the holy ground and the holy people of that urban setting. To me it seemed that they know there is a very thin, yet permeable, separation between the place in which they live and the heaven they ultimately seek. Aware of the spiritual connection between this place and God's heart, they have made their church a place of healing and wholeness.

I left reminded that goodness and shalom emanate out of Iona, out of intercity Glasgow, out of the rural village in which I live, and out of a hundred thousand seemingly unloved and undervalued places that share nothing in common except for one thing: to God they are holy ground. This is deep, green, spiritual sense, God's gift imparted to us through the Celtic expression of Christianity.

CHAPTER 2

ℋoly boy, holy journey

*The lover in the Irish folk song bids his beloved come
with him into the woods, and see the salmon leap in
the rivers, and hear the cuckoo sing, because death
will never find them in the heart of the woods. Oisin,
new come from his three hundred years of faeryland,
and of the love that is in faeryland, bids St. Patrick
cease his prayers a while and listen to the blackbird,
because it is the blackbird of Darrycarn that Fionn
brought from Norway, three hundred years before,
and set its nest upon the oak tree with his own hands.
Surely if one goes far enough into the woods, there
one will find all that one is seeking?*

—*W. B. Yeats*
W. B. Yeats: Writings on Irish Folklore,
Legend and Myth

It is morning. Dew hangs heavy on the grass. The seaside
village of Bannavem Taberniae, on the western coast of
what would one day be called England, has just begun to
stir. The year is roughly 405 C.E. A youth named Patrick,
not quite sixteen, stirs from his sleep. He lives in a

gracious home provided by his British father, who works as a tax collector for the occupying Roman forces. Patrick's family is Christian, his grandfather an elder in the church. Unknown to Patrick, danger is looming out in the morning fog.

A shout is heard in the street, followed by loud noises. Suddenly Patrick comes fully awake to the sound of Irish marauders invading his village! They have crossed the narrow Irish Sea in their skin boats, intent on raiding and raping the elegant Roman-Briton homes and businesses. Patrick's family has anticipated this calamity. His parents and siblings flee to the hiding place.

Patrick, however, is slow of foot. A large Irish hand seizes him by the shoulder. The person belonging to the hand shouts, "Do not kill this one—he will make a fine slave!" Before Patrick can take it all in, he finds himself bound and tied. He is rudely thrown into one of the small skin boats and catches but a fleeting glimpse of his burning village as he sails west. He hopes, but is not sure, that the rest of his family made it to safety.

The sea journey is mercifully short. Still bound, Patrick is marched to the northwest coast of Ireland. This is quite literally the end of the world, as he knows it. There his bindings are loosed, for escape from this isolated, rugged area is thought to be impossible. For the next six years Patrick works as a slave shepherd. This is hard work, and Patrick is continually exposed to the cold, damp weather, all the while protecting the sheep from savage beasts. Young Patrick, raised in an upper-class Roman-Briton home, accustomed to fine things and refined ways, learns to survive in this seemingly God-forsaken wilderness. He learns about sheep, about the windy and cold storms that come up quickly and last for days, and about the ways of the hardy people who are his captors. He learns their language, their customs, and their culture. As a slave, Patrick makes his crude home among the Celts.

The ancient Greeks gave the name *Celt* to these imaginative, romantic, and hospitable people who, like curious children, often embraced new ideas and concepts with glee. The word means "strangers." The word *Celt* is pronounced with a hard C, the Boston Celtics notwithstanding. The Celts first became evident about 600 B.C.E. and moved across the northern boundaries of the Roman Empire from Asia Minor to the Iberian Peninsula. (It is noteworthy that the Irish Celts came to be called *Hiberians* by some, while those of Portugal and Spain were designated *Iberians*.) "The Letter of Paul to the Galatians" was written to the Celts in Galatia. Spreading over the next few hundred years throughout what we know today as the British Isles, the Celts settled in Wales, Cornwall, Scotland, England, Brittany, and the Isle of Man. They reached Ireland, whose inhabitants were then called the "Scotti," in 350 B.C.E.

The Celts were a people of a common language, not a common ethnicity. Obviously, since they were

spread over such a large area, they became ethnically mixed. This mixture was compounded by the influx of Viking and British people into Celtic Ireland in the ninth and twelfth centuries respectively. Thus, today's Irish are perhaps the most ethnically mixed nationality in the world.

They did not have a written language. The Irish gave the druids and druidesses, considered to be both wise and learned, the task of preserving information. They did this by committing to memory philosophical, natural, medical, legal, spiritual, political, and military knowledge. For this reason they were sometimes called "the hidden people," since their stored knowledge was hidden in the deep recesses of their minds.

It borders on being a misnomer to speak of a druidic "religion" since Celtic druidism more closely represented a combined broad system of philosophy, economics, law, and belief. A modern-day comparison would be the whole interacting system of democracy, capitalism, constitutional law, and the myriad of faiths we find in the United States. Combined, these disciplines are intriguing, but they are not a religion in the classic sense of the word. So it was with druidism. It was varied and eclectic and also tinged with magic, mysticism, and civil authority. The law the druids administered was known as the Brehon Law. It was not democratic and favored the tribal kings over the poor. The kings also trusted the druids and druidesses to foretell the future. They often relied on the druids and druidesses' use of spiritualism to seek the advice of ghosts.

The pre-Christian Celts were taught by the druids and druidesses to believe in immortality and were, in fact, one of the first peoples to embrace this belief. The number three was mystical for the Celts in their mythology and art. Their druids often organized their collective wisdom into three-statement teachings.

Irish tradition holds that the druids and druidesses were also master magicians and harp players. Thus, druidism was many things. It was philosophy, it was music. It was political, it was natural. It was practical in its medical, legal, and military aspects. It engaged in matters of the human spirit. All of this contributed to the nature of Celtic druidism, a system often misunderstood today because of New Age practitioners who combine bits and pieces of druidism with other beliefs, liturgies, and philosophies.

The Celts in Ireland in the centuries just before and after Christ were a rural people who knew nothing of cities. As we have already seen, Kildare, Brigid's monastery that grew into a city-state, was founded much later in 490 C.E. while the Vikings founded Dublin, Ireland's first planned city, in 841 C.E. Pre-Christian Celts possessed a oneness with nature that resulted in their happiness and contentment. The Celts believed that plants, animals, and natural features such as oak trees and wells, even weapons, had an indwelling spirit. In this manner they were not unlike aboriginal Native Americans. The Celtic year was rural in nature, determined by counting the number of nights in a year, combined with the flow of planting, growing, harvesting, and dormant seasons. The following rather charming story from Celtic mythology helps define the Irish Celts as a rurally wise people:

> When the primal Celtic tribe of Tuatha de Danaan first established their people in Ireland, Bres, the leader of the former inhabitants of the land, offered them a continual harvest. They refused him, replying,
>
> > This has been our way:
> > Spring for plowing and for sowing,
> > Summer for strengthening the crop,
> > Autumn for grain's ripeness and for reaping,
> > Winter for consuming its goodness.
>
> If we respect the gifts of each season, we will also find the thresholds and doorways of the spirit.[1]

The Celts practiced a tribal form of living. They faithfully took care of the poor, old, and incapable of any age. Unlike many early cultures, they did not practice infanticide—the killing of weak, ill, or disabled infants. The Celts also followed a primitive health-care system that included the eating of nourishing food. When a person died, his debts ceased; thus they did not burden the surviving family. No Celt owned land by himself or herself. This valuable resource was held in common.

The Celts, like many other cultures, did keep slaves. Many of the slaves were children who were sold by their parents into slavery during hard times and famine and children whose parents were killed in war. Typically these slaves were more like indentured servants; they were allowed to leave after serving for a required number of years.

Women and men were equals in Celtic culture, with women afforded full rights and responsibilities, including engaging in war when necessary. In battle the Celts were regarded as fierce fighters who went into combat naked except for twisted, golden necklaces called *torcs*. They frightened their enemies by blowing large, curved trumpets that made a fearsome sound. Celtic bravery was the essence of many myths both the Celts and their enemies created.

This people, divided as they were into tribes, were often prone to arguments resulting in fierce inter-Celtic battles. Their rather ingenious solution to this was to develop the practice of fosterage. The key principle in fosterage was the exchange of children, often firstborn, between tribes. The tribes raised these as beloved adopted children of their own. The result, a unique form of peace-keeping, was that the tribes thought twice about warring among themselves when the result might be killing their own children. Fosterage was also a vehicle for sharing knowledge.

Storytelling was important to the ancient Celts, and it meant more than just relating facts. Good storytelling required artfully spinning tales that grew as each person told them. They considered the words themselves re-markable and precious, indeed, almost sacred. The stories often focused on light, another powerful symbol to these people who lived in a northern gloomy climate.

Celtic culture was imaginative, thoughtful, and creative. It sprang from the heart more than the mind, the soul more than the intellect.

It is in this Celtic culture that Patrick finds himself. Watching and listening, he begins to learn from those around him. Patrick becomes a student of human behavior, quickly noting cues regarding matters of language, social interaction, beliefs, values, and economics. And confronted with captivity, Patrick soon turns to God in fervent prayer. He begins to rediscover his family's Christian faith. He learns to trust God.

Several years later, one night while he is praying, Patrick hears a voice saying, "Your ship is ready." Patrick understands this to be the voice of God telling him that he can finally make his way back to his home and his family.

Incredibly, given the distance and the primitive, dangerous condition of this verdant island, that is exactly what Patrick does. He simply walks away from his flock, eventually missed, but miraculously not apprehended. Patrick travels by foot almost two hundred miles to the east coast of Ireland and persuades a sea captain to take him on board. The captain, the sailors, a cargo of highly prized Irish wolfhounds, and Patrick sail east, probably landing in present-day Wales. From there they set out on foot for twenty-eight days across the country. No doubt the precious cargo of giant wolfhounds consume a large share of the men's provisions. Eventually they run out of food and come near to starvation.

The terrible hunger drives Patrick to prayer once again. God answers by sending a herd of pigs. In time, Patrick reaches home, where his astonished but grateful parents and family welcome him. They had never expected to see him again.

Patrick does not forget the lessons of faith he

learned during his enslavement and travels. He remains prayerful and watchful. Eventually, he has a dream in which he hears the Irish people call out to him, "Holy boy, we ask you to come and walk among us once again." He trains for the priesthood and is ordained. Patrick returns to Ireland, haunted by the memory of his pagan Celtic captors. He understands that their souls have need of Christ. Patrick also literally interprets the message of Acts 1:6–8, believing that if he will take the gospel "to the ends of earth" that Christ will return. For Patrick, western Ireland was geographically and theologically the end of the earth. His mission is inspired by his self-understanding that destiny has led him to fulfill this apocalyptic mission. This self-understanding gives him both power and determination.

But Patrick understands something else that is even more essential to his mission. When he was captive he did not surrender to despair. He kept seeking understanding and hope through his Christian faith and through closely observing everything around him. Thus, as he undertakes his mission of evangelism to Ireland, Patrick understands the culture of the people among whom he was a slave. He knows the language of the farmer who dwells in that land. Undoubtedly, he understands them because he listened to them throughout his years of captivity.

Patrick speaks their language, not just the syllables and words, but the language of their lives and beliefs. So he is able to skillfully interpret the Christian faith to the pagan Celts. To these people who love stories and words, Patrick reads the opening words from the Gospel of John: "In the beginning was the Word, and the Word was with God, and the Word was God. . . . In him was life, and the life was the light of all people. The light shines in the darkness" (John 1:1, 4–5).

Patrick, knowing that these people understand the great dependency sheep have upon shepherds, tells them about Jesus, the Great Shepherd. "I am the good shepherd; I know my sheep and my sheep know me—just as the Father knows me and I know the Father—and I lay down my life for the sheep" (John 10:14, NIV).

The Celts are also known for their hospitality to their Celtic kin and neighbors. Thus, they resonate strongly with the words Patrick reads from Hebrews: "Do not neglect to show hospitality to strangers, for by doing that some have entertained angels without knowing it" (Heb. 13:2).

The druids, guardians of the law and wisdom of the Celts and great lovers of trees which they believed to be sacred, respond with open spiritual curiosity to Patrick's recitation of Psalm 1:1–3:

> Happy are those
> > who do not follow the advice of the wicked,
> > or take the path that sinners tread,
> > > or sit in the seat of scoffers;

but their delight is in the law of the LORD,
and on this law they meditate day and night.
They are like trees
planted by streams of water,
which yield their fruit in its season,
and their leaves do not wither.
In all that they do, they prosper.

Patrick's skillful teaching and the many parallels between his Christian beliefs and their innate ones captivate the Celts. A people who celebrate oneness with creation, they listen attentively to the first chapter of Genesis. Grounded as they are in the rhythms of the agricultural year, they are entranced by tales of a long-ago and faraway rabbi who spins out God's truth in images of seeds, planting, and harvest. As Patrick relates this rabbi's sacrifice of life and the miracle of his resurrection, he enhances their belief in immortality.

These holistic, community-minded Celts cannot resist the allure of a God who promises a jubilee of forgiveness and restoration (Lev. 25) and a time when God will pour out the Spirit "upon all flesh," causing sons and daughters to prophesy, young men to see visions, and old men to dream dreams (Acts 2:17).

These Celts for whom the number three holds mystical meaning are enthralled with Patrick's tale of a God known through the Father, Son, and Spirit. Their brave Celtic warriors, who create peace through fosterage, respond with affirmation to this new faith where peace-makers are blessed, God adopts children into his family, and hope dwells secure.

As F. Delaney has observed, "Many of the impulses and the symbols of Celtic paganism received answer in Christianity."[2] In fact, it is both surprising and amazing how quickly the Celts embrace Christianity, albeit in their own peculiar style. Remarkably, Ireland becomes the first area of Europe to be converted to Christianity without the sacrifice or need for martyrs. This is the legacy of Patrick, who left behind ample written documentation of his existence: an autobiographical statement entitled *Confession* and an epistle protesting slavery entitled *Patrick's Letter against the Soldiers of Coroticus.* The color-ful legends about snakes and shamrocks came later and are probably just those—mere legends.

Centuries later W. B. Yeats, the Irish poet, would write of Patrick and Oisín.[3] Yeats, whose interests ran from the supernatural to Eastern religions, was not a Christian in any conventional sense of the word. Nevertheless, he was steeped in Celtic thought as well as Christian insights, with both being frequent themes in his writings. Therefore, his comments about Patrick and Oisín are insightful and worth considering. Oisín is traditionally known as a bard, an Irish epic poet similar to Homer, whose satire was dreaded and whose praise was revered. His father, Fion, was the traditional dragon-killer of Ireland. Oisín was reputed to have visited the Land of the

Young, a kind of Irish underworld, and tradition says that he told Patrick of this place.

The mention of druids, druidesses, bards, dragon-killers, and the Irish underworld may make the Christian reader a bit nervous, and well it should. As a Christian pastor, writer, and teacher I am admittedly concerned with matters of doctrine. The apostle Paul's words of admonition to Timothy are as important today as they were almost two thousand years ago: "Pay close attention to yourself and to your teaching" (1 Tim. 4:16). We must both teach and believe the gospel continually and accurately.

Still, there is a part of me that is fearful of shutting out theological perspectives that are new and different. Like the Greek philosophers who heard Paul preach in the Areopagus in Athens (Acts 17), I want the opportunity to hear and evaluate, and hear again, if necessary, for clarity. The Celts, who honored hospitality, were also theologically hospitable. As we shall see, their embrace of Christianity provided the world with a uniquely rich thread in the worldwide tapestry of Christian faith and expression. This would not have happened if they had been close-minded.

And so I believe we should consider why Yeats would have Oisín bid Patrick pause from praying so that he might listen to the blackbird. A blackbird? What is inspirational or comforting about the blackbird's "kruck, kruck, kruck"? Precisely nothing. That is the point. The blackbird, scavenger of carrion, cackles a haunting sound that stabs the heart, unlike the sound of the songbird which soothes the soul. To listen to the blackbird is to listen to the emptiness of the human experience. To listen to the blackbird is a journey into the deep, ominous woods where little light penetrates.

Yeats then proceeds to ask a provocative question: "Surely if one goes far enough into the woods, there one will find all that one is seeking?" It is a quintessential Celtic question, grounded in the Celts' deep reverence for what they understood to be sacred groves. And yet, given Yeats's urging that we consider Patrick's journey into the unknown, the paradox is that in their encounter with Patrick and his holy mission, the Celts themselves discovered a deeper spirituality than they had ever imagined possible. Their discovery was beyond woods, beyond blackbirds. They discovered the heart of God as experienced in the Christian faith.

Patrick, of course, also discovered a deeper experience of the Christian faith than he had known as a child. As a boy, Patrick was probably as normal as any other young man. In fact, he wrote his *Confession* in explanation of a serious youthful transgression, not identified, which Patrick had admitted to a Christian friend some time before he was kidnapped. After he became well known because of his mission to Ireland, his former friend turned on him and used the confession to smear Patrick. By then, however, Patrick was no longer the young, sinful boy. When Patrick was stolen away from his family he was also forced to examine his heart. This became for him a holy journey, a pilgrimage not of his own seeking but one that radically changed his life and the lives of countless others.

Patrick could have given up on the western edge of Ireland, but instead he chose to place his hope in the One who sets captives free. Alone, afraid, cold, and hungry he reached out to God's holy presence. God spoke to him in a vision first saying, "You will soon return to your own country," and then, "Your ship is ready." And years later, God spoke to him through another vision in which his former captives called him back. And so, once more the holy boy set out on a holy journey.

Our lives are so often like Patrick's story. We think we are going in one direction and find ourselves pulled in another. We seek a few calm weeks but find ourselves in the midst of turmoil. We plan a celebration for a loved one but find ourselves instead attending the funeral of another. We prepare for a special journey but then find ourselves on the sick bed. Our experience in these times reflects the haunting words Jesus spoke to Peter: "Very truly, I tell you, when you were younger, you used to fasten your own belt and go wherever you wished. But when you grow old, you will stretch out your hands, and someone else will fasten a belt around you and take you where you do not wish to go" (John 21:18).

Our journeys, like Patrick's, often take us where

we do not wish to go. We also face the challenge to "listen to the blackbird." When traversing these paths we are faced with two choices: to succumb to despair or to persevere in faith. One choice is damnation. The other choice leads to the holy ground we are seeking.

CHAPTER 3

*L*EAPING DEER AND WILD GEESE

The ancient pagan Celts knew nothing of temples: enclosed structures by which they might confine and limit the Divine. Even the giant dolmens, huge pillar-like stones supporting pavilion-like "roofs" made of large flat stones, were not places designed primarily for worship. Rather, they were burial places. Other standing stones were most likely shrines to various deities. For the Christian Celts, the place for worship was located in the midst of all they saw around them: flowers, trees, clouds, sky, and all creatures great and small. Woods, wells, and stones were sacred to them. Celtic life was grounded in the beauty and totality of creation.

> In the Celtic understanding of God, the world belongs to God and is sacred because it was created by God. Earth and heaven, nature and grace, light and darkness, the visible and the invisible, belong together. There is a real feeling for nature and confidence in the power of God which cares for all living creatures including the plants and animals. Christianity absorbed this love of nature which was strongly present in Druidic religion.[1]

With these words Marcus Losack and Michael Rodgers, spiritual pilgrimage directors at Glendalough, a Celtic Christian monastic site, expertly define the Celtic understanding of God and creation. The "love of nature" they mention was, however, already an integral part of Christianity long before Patrick and others came to live among the Celts. This is clearly expressed both in Genesis 1:31 ("God saw everything that he had made, and indeed, it was very good"), as well as sung in the nature rhapsody of the psalmist (Psalm 104). Christians did not need the Celtic druids to teach them to love God's creation. They simply needed to be reminded of it.

Likewise, eco-theologian Matthew Fox and others in recent years have reminded and urged the Christian community to renew its spiritual commitment to God's created world. Some have heeded this urging, but many ignore it, often chastising those who do for being "tree-huggers." I think of one denominational executive, an ordained person, whose work took her on frequent trips through rural countryside. Her rather caustic remark was that one would need to have a degree in ornithology (the study of birds) to find these travels interesting.

The early Celtic Christian monks, like their Celtic druid forebears, found great meaning in all of creation. The animals they saw reminded them of God's Story. Perhaps the finest expression of this is found in *The Book of Kells*, a hand-copied and illustrated version of the Gospels which was created by monks on Iona in about the eighth century. Exquisite paintings, called illuminations, adorn each Gospel. The illuminations, executed in the traditional Celtic interweaving scroll and ribbon style, are lavishly portrayed in black, red, purple, yellow, blue, green, and gold. As on this book's cover, a man symbolizes Matthew, to remind us of Jesus' humanity, a lion symbolizes Mark to emphasize the power of the resurrection, a calf symbolizes Luke to highlight the sacrifice of the Christ, and an eagle symbolizes John to accent the Christ's ascension to heaven.

A fish in *The Book of Kells*, as well as in other illuminated scripture manuscripts, also symbolizes the Christ. This symbol, which points to the baptism of the Christ and his call to everyday fishermen to become fishers of men, is rooted in the Greek word for fish, *ichthus*, the first letters of which form an acronym for the Greek words, "Jesus Christ, Son of God, Saviour." The Celtic Christians also, surprisingly, used a snake to symbolize Christ, as it is an animal that sheds its skin to live again. The Celtic Christians were also fond of the lion, since it reminded them that Jesus was "the Lion of the tribe of Judah" (Rev. 5:5). Even the peacock spoke to the Celtic Christians as an animal whose flesh was reported not to putrefy, thus reminding them of everlasting life. They appreciated other animals simply for being part of God's creation: otters, mice, moths, cats, roosters and hens, hounds, goats, wolves, and stags. The early Celtic Christians wove this expanded menagerie into their

illuminated manuscripts. One rather humorous example found in the beautifully illuminated *Book of Kells* is a monastery cat bounding after a mouse that has stolen an Eucharistic wafer.

Today we have a tendency to think about animals in ways that have nothing to do with faith. Powerful buffalo, flaming cardinals, and even the mystical dolphins are reduced to mere athletic mascots. The closest many folks ever come to seeing a stag, fawn, or doe in the wild is in an animated movie. Often people routinely pursue game animals and fish, at best, for their trophy potential and, at worst, simply for the experience of the kill. It is the rare person today who views animals such as these for their spiritual meaning. And yet it was God who created the grace of the deer and the beauty of the pheasant.

My father was not someone whom I considered to be overtly spiritual. However, one incident in his life has repeatedly checked my heart-memory. Dad was an expert shot with a gun. Often, with the aid of a variety of hunting dogs, he brought home rabbits, pheasants, and ducks. And though he invested considerable time deer hunting each year, he never returned with a buck or doe. Our family teased him about this, somewhat unmercifully, until finally one year he brought home a young buck, just large enough to have the legally required antlers.

At the beginning of the hunting season the following year, Dad asked me if I would like to go deer hunting with him. I was a bit surprised, as I was not a hunter. Moreover, this was not a sport I was about to take up in my mid-twenties. But it seemed important to him, so I agreed to go.

We entered the woods on a warm November Saturday afternoon, hiked deep into the trees, and found a log on which to sit. And sit we did, for hours, as rabbits, birds, and deer wandered in and out of our midst. At the end of the afternoon Dad invited me to shoot the gun. He carefully helped me aim it at a tree and squeeze the trigger. The noise and powerful recoil of the weapon shocked me. He took back the gun, put on the safety, and we hiked out of the woods to the car in silence.

I never teased Dad about not getting a deer after that day. Without a word, he had shared something with me that was mystical and very intimate. Only recently have I realized that what he shared was also deeply spiritual.

Tears come to my eyes as I write these words. These are tears precipitated by coming in touch with things beyond the altar, beyond scripture, beyond church polity and structure. These things are not necessarily better than altar, scripture, and ecclesiastical concerns. They are simply and profoundly different. They are simply and profoundly spiritual. And mysterious.

Recalling this experience helps me understand why the Celts, who already revered the plants, animals, and rocks around them, intertwined these things in their embrace of Christianity. No doubt it helped that the Christians brought with them the psalmist's understanding of God as Creator:

> O LORD, how manifold are your works!
> In wisdom you have made them all;
> the earth is full of your creatures.
>
> (Psalm 104:24)

The Celt in me intertwines the animals I encounter in my travels into my faith and life experience. A doe, frozen by the side of the road with ears high and alert, peering unafraid at me from the tall grass in the wake of a brief thunderstorm, leaves a lasting imprint on my soul. Groundhogs diving for cover remind me of overweight ballet dancers and bring me the gift of laughter. A hawk hungrily tears apart roadkill, boldly ignoring the threat of my speeding auto, a holy boldness of the animal world.

Another hawk, very young, startled me and a bevy of other drivers one day on the expressway. The hawk suddenly swooped down upon a small, unfortunate rodent crouching on the narrow, grassy meridian. In response, six lanes of traffic, three in each direction, threw on their brakes, causing an aurora borealis of red lights. The hawk, oblivious to the screeching vehicles, continued his dive-bomb low across the highway, heading ever downward over three lanes, snatching his prey in mid-flight, and then accelerating and lifting over the other three lanes. It was the most startling exhibition of raw, natural courage (or foolishness!) that I have ever witnessed. Every time I remember the hawk's successful dive in the face of almost certain death, I am still left breathless. What a creature God created in the hawk!

My work takes me over countless roads to over a hundred meetings, about fifty worship services, and countless one-on-one visits a year. I currently serve in an area where my days are blessed with continual vistas of mountains, valleys, trees, streams, and a wide variety of plants and animals. The miles I drive are long, often through inclement weather. I also travel often by airplane and am always enthralled when the weather is clear and I can view rivers, forests, harbors, lakes, and seas from the air. People frequently ask me if I become bored with all my travels for the church. The answer is no, never! There is always so much to see and experience. God stood back from creation on the seventh day, looked at it, and pronounced it good. Creation is our good and holy companion. In its presence there is peace. In its presence there is beauty. In its presence there is hope.

I pity those persons who lack an eye for the creation and the Creator. They miss seeing the encouragement offered in and through creation. Early in my pastoral ministry, I sat one long morning in the home of a parishioner whose college-age daughter was undergoing emergency surgery over a hundred miles away. The mother chose not to rush to her daughter's side, but to stay home in prayer until the surgery was completed. The surgery, not the daughter's first, for she was chronically ill, was very complicated and serious. I was terrified that she might not survive and that the anticipated telephone call from the surgeon would bring terrible news.

God acting through creation saved me that morning. Just outside the picture window of the woman's home several deer grazed for the duration of the surgery. The large stag and his harem slowly ate their way across the woods-bordered lawn. Their long, lingering presence brought calmness upon both the mother and me, which sustained us mightily in that hour. I cannot speak for her—a mother's love never surrenders—but I might well have given up to despair without the presence of those deer. They seemed to me on that day a holy sign, sent to bring great reassurance and deep peace. My soul longed that morning for the reassuring presence of God and the deer caused me to be aware of that presence. Now when I recall that day these words from Psalm 42 always come to mind:

As a deer longs for flowing streams,
    so my soul longs for you, O God. . . .
Why are you cast down, O my soul,
    and why are you disquieted within me?
Hope in God; for I shall again praise him,
    my help and my God.

                    (Psalm 42:1, 11)

To the Irish Celts the sudden experience of God in one's life, be it for the first time or along the journey of faith, is known as "the leap of the deer." There is something in the powerful yet graceful majesty of a deer that reminds the human heart of God. This is what I experienced that day in my parishioner's home.

Birds can do this, too. One day I lay on my back on the island of Staffa, off the west coast of Scotland. As I lay there on the edge of high cliff, a flock of black and white puffins with their comical orange web feet continually cruised the cliff just a couple of feet above my head. It seemed I was part of the soaring flock and it felt both good and holy.

Another bird, the wild goose, is a symbol of the Holy Spirit for the Celtic Christians. This bird, both common and yet magnificent in flight, powerfully reminds them of the Spirit who soars, and swims, and seemingly laughs in the face of trial, temptation, and trepidation. Such a goose surprised me one morning last autumn when I was sitting on the deck of my summer home reading a

book of Celtic Christian prayers. It suddenly flew overhead, honked noisily, and startled me out of my meditative thoughts. It seemed to say, "Close that book and
look around you at the glory of autumn which God has
created." I closed my book, opened my eyes to the
October morning, and celebrated the presence of the
Holy Spirit.

My denomination's newest hymnal contains the
chorus to a beautiful song, "On Eagle's Wings." It has
quickly become a favorite, loved at all times and often
requested for funerals. I heard it sung on the televised
memorial service for the Oklahoma City bombing victims'
families and it spoke to my heart that day. Its words,
inspired by Exodus 19:4, are a celebration of the
sustaining power of God through creation.

> And God will raise you up on eagle's wings,
> Bear you on the breath of dawn,
> Make you to shine like the sun,
> And hold you in the palm of God's hand.*

The blessed assurance of these words, expressed in
beautiful imagery, is rooted in God acting through
creation and on behalf of humanity. Only the nature of
God is divine, but creation, the product of God's hand, is
both sacred and holy because it belongs to God.

* "On Eagle's Wings" © 1979, 1991, New Dawn Music, 5536 NE
Hassalo, Portland, OR 97213. All rights reserved. Used with permission.

The earth is the LORD's and all that is in it,
    the world, and those who live in it;
for he has founded it on the seas,
    and established it on the rivers.
Who shall ascend the hill of the LORD?
    And who shall stand in his holy place?

            (Psalm 24:1–3)

Ours is a God who did not create this world on a whim, but rather for a saving, redeeming purpose: that we might know God through creation. This, however, is no mere pantheistic deity. For God so loved creation that God sent the Son into it for its peoples and for their souls.

And the Spirit, whether we think of it as a white dove or a wild goose, hovers over the holy ground of creation, breathing life and vitality into it, into you, and into me.

CHAPTER 4

*T*URNING DARKNESS INTO LIGHT

A monk sits at a crude wooden table. Before him lies a piece of ruled vellum made from a much-refined calfskin. Next to the vellum lies another sheet with Greek words written on it. He picks up a quill pen and begins to copy the Gospel of Mark. He works slowly, but deliberately and with much thought. Periodically he lays down the pen he uses to copy the words in reddish-brown ink and picks up fur brushes dipped in brilliant colors. With these he decorates, or illuminates, the sentences with colorful drawings depicting animals, plants, other monks, fanciful shapes, and biblical characters.

Copying the scriptures consumes the monk's days. But there is not much else for this monk to do on the rocky island which is his home, except to grow just enough food to survive, coupled with his community's fishing, and to attend to the private and public worship of God. Copying manuscripts is the main focus of his life. The monk focuses on the Word and the Word focuses his body, mind, and spirit.

Once in a while a bit of whimsy comes over him,

and he turns his attention from scripture copying to poetry writing. He is, after all, a wordsmith. One recent poem he shared with his fellow monks. They found it both amusing and at the same time, a winsome testimony to their shared labor. The poem the monk writes in the margins of the text he is copying compares his literary diligence to the physical disciplines of his cat:

> I and Pangur Ban my cat,
> 'Tis a like task we are at:
> Hunting mice is his delight,
> Hunting words I sit all night.
>
> 'Tis a merry thing to see
> At our tasks how glad are we,
> When at home we sit and find
> Entertainment to our mind.
>
> 'Gainst the wall he sets his eye,
> Full and fierce and sharp and sly;
> 'Gainst the wall of knowledge I
> All my little wisdom try.
>
> So in peace our task we ply,
> Pangur Ban my cat and I;
> In our arts we find our bliss,
> I have mine and he has his.

Practice every day has made
Pangur perfect in his trade.
I get wisdom day and night
Turning darkness into light.[1]

During the Dark Ages, while the rest of Europe languished under the invasion of the Visigoths and the fall of the Roman Empire, Celtic Christianity flourished in its own Golden Age. This was the time when Celtic monks served as prodigious scribes, making extensive copies not only of the Christian scriptures but also of Latin and Greek literature. They fashioned the words in the distinctive Celtic curved Hebrew and Greek script, then illustrated these manuscripts with colorful illuminations. As the Dark Ages waned and came to conclusion, it was the Celtic Christians who largely reintroduced Christian and other classical literature into Europe. They preserved the Word so that they could return its light to places where it had been almost entirely extinguished. Celtic Christian monks and priests hand carried the scriptures back into Northern Europe, traveling up great rivers such as the Rhine. They established monasteries in places as far away as Switzerland. Visitors to Saint Gall, Switzerland, can today view elaborate Celtic Christian illuminated manuscripts in the monastery museum located in that city.

The task of copying the ancient manuscripts by hand—word by word, line by line, paragraph by paragraph—was enormous. The intricate and vivid drawings,

many utilizing Celtic motifs such as knots, circles, animals, and plants, were elaborate, stylized, and ornate. They were also occasionally humorous. Some manuscripts feature delightful pictures of monks pulling each other's beards, animals chasing each other's tails, and two mice fighting over the Eucharistic bread. That these Celtic Christian monks could intertwine their droll comics as adornments with the sacred scriptures is a delightful wonder of God. These illuminations told the reader much about the monks' understanding of God, the Creator of artistic shapes, animals, plants, humanity, and even laughter. These drawings, in reality, illuminated and shed light upon these ancient words: "Your word is a lamp to my feet and a light to my path" (Psalm 119:105).

Even in the graphic-laden, multimedia age in which we live, these manuscripts radiate a complexity and beauty that captures both the imagination and the heart.

Truly God gifted the monks who created these manuscripts with creativity, talent, and dedication. And the
amazing thing is that God found the right people to do
this work at precisely the time in Christian history when
they were badly needed. Or maybe it is not so amazing;
maybe it was God, who always loves a good story, just
being God.

The Celtic Christians who created the great
illuminated manuscripts were mostly Irish. Words have
always had great power for the Irish people. Thomas
Cahill, in his masterful recent bestseller, *How the Irish
Saved Civilization*, notes that the Celtic Christian monks'
preservation of the Christian scriptures (including the
Apocrypha) and ancient Greek and Roman literature
revealed a key cultural feature: "Even at this early stage in
their development, the Irish were intoxicated by the
power of words."

My travels in pursuit of a deeper understanding of
Celtic Christianity have taken me to many interesting
places. One place, however, is distinctively holy among the
rest: The Chester Beatty Library and Gallery of Oriental
Art in Dublin. Chester Beatty was an American mining
magnate who generously presented his vast collection of
oriental art and his unique collection of religious and
other writings to Ireland, which resulted in his selection as
Ireland's first honorary citizen in 1957. This museum,
itself a testimony to the Irish tendency to be intoxicated
by the power of words, holds 270 copies of the Koran,

six-thousand-year-old Babylonian stone tablets, Greek papyri dating from the second century C.E., and biblical material written in Coptic, the language of Egypt from about the third to the tenth centuries. In addition, the museum includes the *Coëtivy Book of Hours*, an illuminated French prayer book dating from the fifteenth century.

For me the truly enchanting thing about The Chester Beatty Library and Gallery is that it also contains the oldest complete set of the Gospels and the oldest existent fragment of the Gospel of Mark, dating from approximately 200 C.E. These are the printed words of Jesus separated by only 170 years from Jesus himself and approximately 130 years from the author of Mark. For me, viewing these documents was a profound spiritual experience. I found myself repeatedly drawn back to the ancient Gospel manuscripts. I did not want to take my eyes from them. I sensed their mystic connection to the One who "in the beginning was the Word" (John 1:1), the One whose power lies not in might, but in the inexplicable creative energy of the Word.

Although I am a person who typically is deeply moved by encounters with land (holy ground), in this case it was words that held me spellbound. Even a visit I made to the Holy Land twelve years ago did not captivate me as these manuscripts did. In my mind I tried to calculate how few or many hands might have touched the manuscripts, thus trying to determine just how many actual persons stood between my experience of them and the mouth of the One whose words they recorded. Standing in their presence, I was spiritually elated and emotionally overcome. It was a most difficult thing for me when time finally demanded that I pull myself away from them and leave the museum.

As a child I was taught the hymn, "I Love to Tell the Story." The Story, of course, is the biblical story of God's love. It is indeed more precious than "all my golden fancies of all my golden dreams." And yet, the tendency is to take the Story for granted, especially when we find it all around us in plenteous forms including a multitude of translations printed on CD-ROM. In the time in which we live, accessing the Story is a fairly simple act. One wonders if the seeming overabundance of biblical resources, available even at the grocery checkout, does not in some way diminish, rather than enhance, the precious nature of the Story.

Even more worrisome is the proliferation of so-called New Age literature that often represents a synthesis of various world religions and humanistic writings. Is there a hidden danger in the blizzard of spiritually oriented written materials available to us today? Does this profusion somehow obscure the miraculous nature of the essential Word, as contained in the Christian scriptures, to lead, guide, and transform human lives? Does this cause us to take the Word too casually?

Some, to be sure, do not take the Word casually. In the early part of the 1990s I worked for three and half years in the Western Jurisdiction of The United Methodist Church. The first time I visited the Yellowstone Conference, consisting of churches in Montana and northern Idaho, I was told to reserve judgment if I heard pastors reading slowly from the Bible. I understood this to mean that the reading levels of folks in that remote region were not as high as in other places. Much to my surprise, however, when I did hear some pastors reading the scriptures aloud at a decidedly slow pace, I discovered that it was not because of their inability to read English well. Rather, those pastors were reading directly from the Hebrew and Greek texts! These were pastors who took the Story seriously, and in their own way they were as meticulous in their study of it as those Irish monks who carefully copied and illuminated manuscripts.

Today the opportunities for searching the scriptures are limited only by technological ignorance. While their tools may seem primitive by our standards, the Celtic monks' vellum, pens, brushes, inks, and paints were the "high tech" tools of their day. Like those unnamed but wise monks, we need to make good use of the technology that is available to us in our own time. We should value that technology as a gift from God in the same way those Celtic Christians revered the tools that enabled them to do the work of "turning darkness into light."

Remember those pastors in Montana? They were the first people I knew who were "surfing the Net," using computers to communicate via the Internet. Like them, Christians are surfing the Net today and finding Bible study resources, biblical archeological reviews, and "chat rooms" where they can discuss the scriptures and their own spiritual journeys via e-mail. Their fascination with the Word of God finds expression in technology, and who is to say this is not a gift from God?

Nevertheless, biblical literacy is not intended to be a private affair. Just as those monks shared the Word of God with Europe as it emerged from the Dark Ages, we are called to share it with others who live in darkness. I am grateful to Bishop Hae-Jong Kim, who has helped me to see the connection between what he calls "the text" and "the context." Bishop Kim's point is that we must first understand, embrace, and believe the text with all of our heart, soul, and mind. Then we must diligently work at telling the text in such a way that it relates to the context of the hearer. This is what turns darkness into light, what illuminates the dark corners of the human soul wherever that soul happens to be.

It is important to remember that the Celts, a people whose very nature was "intoxicated by words," were a people who loved great stories and that the stories had unique meaning for their lives. Their stories told of how the Celtic people came to be, why they planted and harvested at certain times of the year, and of the great battles they had fought and won. These were romantic, brave, mystical tales. It is no surprise that when Patrick came linking their story to the gospel Story, as we saw earlier in this book, they embraced his Spirit-filled tales with enthusiasm.

Not long ago I took a group of seminary students on a three-day "rural plunge." During this time they visited a large dairy farm, two mining areas, and several villages. They listened to folks describe the economic and social aspects of their communities. Members of rural congregations shared with these seminarians, many of whom were students from urban areas, how they live and minister in the place where they find themselves.

In one church, several members of the congregation laid it on thick about how high the snow gets each winter and how far they live from stores, most jobs, and other services. Finally, one retired dairy farmer stood up and told the class the "tall tale" of the place God created for him and his family to live. He spoke of a high hill outside of town where "You can reach up at night and turn the moon on brighter for more light and where, if the snow is too deep, the wind simply comes and blows it all away." The poetry of his words revealed a love of the place where his life story has been played out. Intoxicated by the words he spoke, this man revealed his understanding of the God who created that place for him and others who love it, too. This layman was turning darkness into light right before our eyes. It was not a difficult leap in my mind from this farmer's words to the words of the psalmist:

O LORD, our Sovereign,
how majestic is your name in all the earth! . . .
When I look at your heavens, the work of your fingers,
the moon and the stars that you have
established;
what are human beings that you are mindful of them,
mortals that you care for them?

(Psalm 8:1, 3–4)

Instantly a sermon began to form in my mind, a sermon written upon the holy ground—the story place— of this spiritually wise man's experience of life and God. I have not finished that sermon yet. But when I do, it will be a good one.

I get wisdom day and night,
Turning darkness into light.

$\mathcal{S}$MOORING THE FIRE

A woman bends over the hearth in her home. It is late evening and she is about to retire for the night. But first she must accomplish an important task, the smooring of the fire. She carefully banks the red-hot coals of the fire, arranging them in a circle and then dividing them into three parts. As she does this she gives thanks for the presence of the Trinity: God the Father, God the Son, and God the Holy Spirit.

Early tomorrow morning she will rekindle flame from the coals. She will use peat to build a roaring fire from which she will extract more red-hot coals. These she will place in a metal container and carry through the foggy sunrise to her daughter's new home. Her daughter will be married tomorrow, and the coals, the smoored fire, are her mother's precious wedding gift to her.

This fire has been in the family for a long time, literally hundreds of years. Generation after generation of women has smoored the fire, each mother passing it on to her daughter on her wedding day. In a damp climate where tending a fire is constant work, these are precious family heirlooms. In them we find the ancient Celtic

tradition of smooring the fire, keeping it, and passing it on to those who need it.

Fire always had great meaning for the pagan Celts. An important annual tradition was the lighting of the springtime Beltane bonfire by the druids, who acted under the supervision of the Irish high king. Common law held that no one, under pain of death, could light his or her bonfire before the high king lit his. This event always took place on Tara, a political and spiritual center of Celtic Ireland and the seat of the high kings until the eleventh century. On a clear day much of Ireland can be viewed from this high flat hill, which provides a full 360-degree viewing radius.

From Tara looking across the plains of County Meath, one can view Slane Hill, whose hymn tune, "Slane," is usually sung with the eighth- or ninth-century Irish text, "Be Thou My Vision." In 433 C.E. Patrick lit an Easter bonfire on Slane Hill just as the high king was preparing to light his. This was an act of open defiance. The dangerous point Patrick made was that the fire symbolizing the resurrection of Christ supersedes any other fire.

The scene that followed is somewhat reminiscent of the story of Elijah as told in 1 Kings 18, where the prophet openly defied the pagan agricultural Baal priests on Mount Carmel, literally slaying them with his pyrotechnics. Patrick, however, was of a more merciful bent. When the high king from Tara roared up with his twenty-two chariots and two powerful wizards, ready to slay this fire-lighting upstart, Patrick countered with the words of a psalm: "Some take pride in chariots, and some in horses, but our pride is in the name of the LORD our God" (Psalm 20:7).

That was enough for one of the king's men, Eric, to succumb to the intoxication of the Word and the grace of God. Eric converted to Christianity on the spot. The wizards tried a bit more of their razzle-dazzle (casting of spells and chanting incantations) on Patrick, but to no avail. They eventually surrendered to the grace of God. At last even the high king submitted to conversion, saying, "It is better for me to believe than to die." Although the words from the psalm had certainly stopped the high king and his men in their tracks, some say it was the power and breath of the words engraved on Patrick's breastplate that intoxicated the high king with the spirit of God:

> I arise today
> Through a mighty strength, the invocation of the Trinity,
> Through belief in the threeness,
> Through confession of the oneness
> Of the Creator of Creation. . . .

I arise today
Through the strength of heaven:
Light of sun,
Radiance of moon,
Splendor of fire.[1]

The words *splendor of fire* have been variously translated as "and fire with all the strength it hath,"[2] "fire's glory,"[3] and "the flashing of the lightning free."[4] These words, attributed by legend to Patrick, are part of a larger prayer known as "St. Patrick's Breastplate Prayer." Breastplate prayers were a common prayer form in the early centuries of Celtic Christianity. They symbolized the protection afforded by the trinitarian God. Patrick's prayer describes that protection as all-encompassing, totally surrounding him. And fire was an important component of that circling presence of God. This was fire, with all its splendor, strength, glory, and freedom. This was fire, to be kept, nurtured, and honored.

The Christian faith is always in need of smooring. The fire needs to be kindled and rekindled if it is to be there for the next generation. Hard times that challenge our faith and threaten to extinguish the fire come and go. If the faith is not preserved today like precious fire, it may not be there for tomorrow's children.

My father's parents were not Christian people. In fact, almost no one on his side of the family had or has any church ties. Through historical research I have been able to imagine a scenario that may have caused this. Dad's grandfather came from Ireland not long after the terrible Potato Famine of the late 1840s (known as the "Great Hunger" among the Irish people). Quite possibly his family had an active Christian faith before this frightening time of hunger, sickness, and death. They may well have joined the thousands of Irish citizenry who became so angry with God during this time that they quite literally lost their faith.

Another possibility is that they simply became entangled and frustrated with the ongoing Catholic and Protestant friction within the country. This may have caused them to cease believing in either expression of the Christian faith.

Yet another possible explanation stems from the Irish having maintained through the centuries a strong cultural embrace of folklore, legend, and myth fixated upon faeries, ghosts, banshees (spirit women whose shrieks accompanied human death), and other assorted creatures of the spirit world. This cultural legacy could have intertwined with their practice of the Christian faith to the point where it became difficult, if not impossible, to discern one from the other.

And then perhaps, facing discrimination in this country because they were impoverished Irish people, they simply abandoned their native faith in an effort to be assimilated into their new culture. In the midst of this faith confusion, coals that once burned brightly somehow dimmed and cooled.

And yet, something spiritual remained in my father, who practiced a remnant form of partial agnosticism that evidently had been passed through the generations in his family. Dad had faith, but not much. I am reminded that *yether* is the Hebrew word for "remnant" and it means "what is left." There simply was not much faith left.

When I search my memory, I am reminded that my father regularly observed one annual, quasiliturgical event. When the firstfruits of the family garden appeared around August first, Dad would scoop them up into his arms and come into the house singing,

> Bringing in the sheaves,
> Bringing in the sheaves,
> We shall come rejoicing,
> Bringing in the sheaves.

My mother, a committed Christian, and I were always a bit startled by this sudden appearance of hymnodic religiosity on my father's part. And as far as she and I know, that was the only hymn he knew, except for "The Old Rugged Cross." That was his mother's favorite hymn, although she did not actively practice Christianity either.

I am haunted by this memory of a remnant

spirituality that my father evidently inherited. Ultimately the decision not to seek a more defined faith was his, but I cannot help but pity him because the coals he inherited were too cold to be easily fanned into flame.

I worshiped one day at St. Patrick's Cathedral in Dublin, the national cathedral of the Protestant church in Ireland. The liturgy was Anglican. Once again the earnest plea was made: "Lord, have mercy. Christ, have mercy, Lord, have mercy." Mercy on what? Our souls, of course. The very core of our being. That spiritual spark that makes each of us who we are.

I fear that we do not tend those spiritual sparks as we should. We are not as soul-conscious as we should be. I often do workshops at various sites around the United States focusing on how churches can hone their ministries with a biblically based model of nurture, outreach, and witness. In the workshops I frequently use the word *soul* when talking about the concept of praying for individuals whose souls we know and understand to be without faith. I am amazed by how many participants in these workshops, both laity and clergy alike, tell me that they have not heard anyone in organized religion refer to the term *soul* in years, if not decades. This is surprising, as there have been some recent well-written books about the concept of the soul. Evidently the wider church has yet to embrace the significance of this aspect of Christianity.

We have forgotten much. The pagan Celts had a focused sense of soul, searching for means to enliven and quicken it through meditative intercourse with plants and animals, the seasons, and their hero gods. Even their characteristic fascination with circular drawings, which probably signified their sense of the wholeness and holiness of life, contained a sense of soul. The Celtic Christians joined together the Celtic circular design with the powerful Christian cross symbol, creating the ringed cross. It is a soul cross.

Unlike the ancient Celts, we are often soul-negligent, asking for mercy without taking the time to tender the spark of our soul that yearns for the fire of God. Frequently we are busy with church matters but neglect the care of our own hearts. We need to be soul-touched, soul-filled, and soul-blessed. The well-tended soul is in touch with its Creator. The fire of the well-tended Christian soul may waiver in times of trial, but smoored by God it cannot be extinguished.

> The soul that on Jesus still leans for repose,
> I will not, I will not desert to its foes;
> That soul, though all hell should endeavor to shake,
> I'll never, no, never, no, never forsake.

Among us are those souls that have grown cold. Those souls, just like yours and mine, are in need of soul tending, just as the flames of a fire need to be carefully tended.

A note of caution: one cannot be casual about this

work of tending the fire without risking danger. A conversation comes to mind which I had one day with a store clerk. We spoke together a few days after yet another tragic shooting event in a rural schoolyard. The clerk shared her fears that her sixteen-year-old son might commit a similar atrocity. She described him as a self-proclaimed atheist and a very angry young man.

I asked about her faith background. She replied she had been raised United Methodist but had married a Roman Catholic man. She agreed to allow him to raise the children in his faith, but a divorce ensued. Neither the woman nor her husband provided religious training for her son and his sister, simply hoping that each child would find a faith in which they were comfortable. Her son at least was thinking about spiritual matters, although denying the existence of God. Her daughter was not interested in the subject at all. Now the mother was frantic that her son might become the next newspaper headline about school shootings.

The irony of our conversation was that while the mother could see the spiritual danger her children faced, she did not recognize how the cooled coals of her own faith were endangering her own soul. What a tragic comparison to the mother whose story of kindled faith began this chapter!

By comparison, a couple in their early twenties came to me a few years ago seeking Christian marriage. Upon inquiry I learned that the young man had sporadically attended church as a child and youth and thus had some basic knowledge of the Christian faith. The bride-to-be was not a Christian and neither were her parents. Unfortunately, her lack of faith formation is more the norm today among children of baby boomers.

After the premarital counseling we talked about the wedding service, including whether or not to use the Lord's Prayer. Not surprisingly, the woman asked, "What is it?" Before I could answer, her fiancé leaned over, patted her hand, and said, "We want it—I'll teach it to you before our wedding day." And he did. The thought of him bringing those lingering coals of his faith to flame and then sharing that flame with his new wife remains a joyful memory in my heart.

It is so easy to let the coals of faith cool and die. We recently went through a spiritually dangerous time in our own household. It began innocently enough. Our family prayers, an important time of sharing, typically were dinner-table prayers and evening prayers which we shared with our family dog. (Now, I do not actually think the dog prayed, but ours seemed to sense an important family moment—a word of encouragement for those with young children who can certainly understand the same! Praying with him also made sense to our creation-centered celebration of God's love and grace.)

When good weather arrived in the spring, we began spending more time at our summer home. A new dinner table, ordered in the winter months, did not arrive in time to replace the old one that we had already sold. We found it unsettling to attempt praying with meals spread out over the coffee table and end table. And then the dog, our beloved family pet, became terminally ill and had to be put down. Our grief was deep with the loss of this good, dear, and faithful friend. Between the loss of the dog and the absence of a dinner table our family prayer life began to unravel. All this was bad enough, but then illness caused us to miss worship on several Sundays.

One Monday morning I woke up exhausted from a weekend of church meetings and worship services. I faced a 175-mile drive to attend a work-related retreat that necessitated my presence. My desk was piled high with unopened mail and correspondence crying for attention. Despair descended upon me. Tears began to flow. I slammed a few doors as I packed and made my way out to the garage. I was frustrated, empty, and physically worn-out.

God and I worked together to smoor the embers of my faith that morning. Spring was in full bloom, the sky was blue, and my drive took me through the beautiful rolling highlands that lay throughout New York's Finger Lakes region. A retreat was the last thing I thought I had time for, but God made the drive worthwhile. By the time I arrived, I was ready for God to help me rebuild my spiritual fires.

The irony of the day was that when I arrived I learned that my attendance had not really been mandatory. But by that time it did not matter. I stayed for two days, enjoying the radiance of the spiritual fires burning inside the hearts of others at the retreat and basking in the splendor of the retreat center's lakeside setting. I left with my own spiritual fires rekindled and having made a commitment to reignite our household's spiritual life.

The story is told of a small-town church that caught fire and burned to the ground. In the aftermath of the fire the pastor found himself walking through the smoldering ruins with the local fire chief. Since the fire chief never attended worship, the pastor could not resist commenting, "Well, I've never seen you in church before!" To which the fire chief replied, "Well, I've never seen the church on fire before!" Churches cannot catch fire unless the embers are tended or smoored.

Jim and Joan, a married couple who are members of a small Christian congregation, are people who understand this. They have seen the vitality of their church wax and wane over almost forty years of church mem-

bership. When times are bad, they do extra duty, pitching in to take on additional leadership roles and dream new dreams of creative ministry for the congregation. With their prayers and service, and with the help of God, they have many times fanned the dimming coals of their congregation back into a roaring fire. The Christian faith needs more people like Jim and Joan.

The history of Christianity can, of course, be traced through a series of times when the fire of Christianity has been rekindled from smoored coals. Tongues of fire on the Day of Pentecost rekindled the hearts and minds of Christ's apostles and disciples. That rekindled fire blazed across the Roman Empire. Celtic Christianity rekindled light in Europe at the end of the Dark Ages. Luther's Reformation set all of Europe on fire with holy, renewed faith.

In eighteenth-century England the fire of Christianity had nearly extinguished for all but the wealthiest persons in much of Ireland, Scotland, and Wales. Destitute miners, the mainstay of the labor force, could not attend church for a variety of reasons, including forced labor on Sunday and the poverty that provided no decent clothing thought fit to wear to church. It was at this point that John Wesley took the smoored fire of Christianity to these miners. Rejecting the formality of high church altars and pulpits, he began to preach in open fields and at the entranceways into the mines. Seeing the colliery fires on the hillsides above the mines, he interpreted them as the smoored fires of God's grace. His brother, Charles, wrote this hymn text to illustrate the unleashing of those fires:

> See how great a flame aspires,
> Kindled by a spark of grace.
> Jesus' love the nations fires,
> Sets the kingdoms on a blaze.
> To bring fire on earth he came,
> Kindled in some hearts it is;
> O that all might catch the flame,
> All partake the glorious bliss!

It is interesting to note that many Celtic Christian scholars view the Wesleys as the natural successors to the Celtic Christian spirit. That spirit had grown dim, but not gone out, during the Late Renaissance of the fifteenth and sixteenth centuries and the beginning of the Age of Reason in the seventeenth and early eighteenth centuries. John Wesley even refers to his Christian conversion as feeling as though his heart had been "strangely warmed." Interesting language, indeed, for one standing in the long line of Celtic Christian heritage!

Jesus said, "I came to bring fire to the earth, and how I wish it were already kindled!" (Luke 12:49) The sweep of this statement is both majestic and challenging. Jesus came to rekindle the fire of the Hebrew faith, a deep, trusting faith in God who alone has the power to save. Even he was frustrated with the barriers he saw to rekindling that fire. It was hard work, but Jesus accomplished the smooring task. When finally he stood on the holy ground of the garden, preparing to depart for the countryside of Galilee, at last the kindling burst into flame. This is why the tradition of lighting vigil fires on Easter Eve, just as Patrick did so long ago, has great meaning for Christian people. These fires are sign and symbol of the resurrection and eternal life of Christ.

On a personal level, Samuel Longfellow's hymn text reflects these resurrection fires:

> Holy Spirit, Love divine,
> Glow within this heart of mine;
> Kindle every high desire;
> Perish self in thy pure fire.

But the Christian faith is never simply a personal experience. This holy ground on which we live is ground shared with the people, plants, animals, hills, and valleys of God's good creation. The fire we kindle is not just for ourselves, but for the very creation in which God has placed us. The fire we kindle is for our lives, our homes, and our world. Like the Celtic Christian woman on her knees praying the following smooring prayer, we, too, kneel together on holy ground and echo her prayer before a holy fire.

The sacred Three,
To save,
To shield,
To surround
The hearth,
The house,
The household,
This eve,
This night,
Oh! this eve,
This night,
And every night,
Each single night.
Amen.[5]

$\mathcal{I}$N THE HOWLING, COMFORTING WILDERNESS

Our lives unfold in cities, on open prairies, in deep forests, among suburban developments, in swampy bayous, in small towns, in rugged mountains, and in a variety of other settings. Our experience of faith, closely linked to the various events and conditions of our lives, often has the feel of a desert or wilderness sojourn. This is usually accompanied by thirst, both spiritual and social. Many people thirst for community, for other human beings who share their interests, passions, and sense of pleasure and fun. These folks are in the desert of loneliness. Other persons, like parched wanderers, search in their surrounding wilderness for economic, racial, ecological, or social justice for themselves and those with whom they minister. Still others find themselves in a wilderness full of subversive violence. These folks seek peace the way a sunburnt desert wanderer seeks cool shade.

The wilderness, however, can also be a place of comfort, where we discover God who always goes, paradoxically, both before and with us. In the wilderness, we discover, we are in God's hands. This is the message that Moses sang to the people of Israel, echoing what God had done for Jacob in the desert:

> He sustained him in a desert land,
>   in a howling wilderness waste;
> he shielded him, cared for him,
>   guarded him as the apple of his eye.
>
> (Deuteronomy 32:10)

When life drives us to the wilderness we must cultivate the ability to trust that God will shelter, feed, protect, and most importantly, be with us in whatever circumstance we find ourselves. Without this trust, cynicism sets in. Despair often follows.

Such trust defies human logic. Catherine de Hueck Doherty's book, *Poustinia*, the title of which is Russian for "desert," explores the desert experience. She writes of the Eastern Christian practice of solitary wilderness retreats, saying: "Since the reason for entering the poustinia is one of listening to God in prayer and fasting, the first act of a poustinik is to fold the wings of his intellect and open the doors of his [sic] heart."

W. B. Yeats, who we have noted was not a Christian writer in the strict sense of the word, reflected the same sentiment when he wrote of his own self-understanding: "I have all-ways considered my self a voice of what I believe to be a greater renaisance [sic]—the revolt of the soul against the intellect—now beginning in the world."[1]

The folding of the wings of the intellect, the opening the doors of the heart, and the revolt of the soul against the intellect describes the vital core of the Celtic Christian experience.

Anthony, a third-century mystic who took to the deserts of Egypt and founded Christian monasticism, had much effect on the early Celtic Christian church. Word and testimony of this Christian lifestyle spread to Martin, who became Bishop of Tours around 370 C.E. So impressed was Martin that he adopted it for himself. Soon a British priest named Ninian came to Marmoutier to spend time with Martin. Ninian, too, adopted the monastic concept. The result was the founding of a monastery at Whithorn (also known as *Candida Casa* or The Pure House) located south of present-day Glasgow. Eventually the faithful at Whithorn launched a mission to Ireland.

Of course, the Celtic Christians in Briton, Ireland, and Scotland had no deserts in which to establish their monasteries. The ancient Celts, however, had long considered the forests to be sacred places and stones and rock formations to hold mystical qualities. So they went to the deep, remote woods and to rugged, rocky, small islands where human life was both difficult and dangerous. (Iona, which I described in chapter 1, is such a place.) Skellig Michael, a rocky island off the west coast of

Ireland, was another such place. Celtic Christian monks lived there from the sixth century, inhabiting small, beehive-shaped stone cells, which offered little shelter from the cold, angry North Atlantic winds. They survived by eating fish and selling bird eggs gathered from high cliff nests to the fishermen who dared to moor near their island.

Glendalough, another early Celtic Christian monastery located in a more beautiful, seemingly lush, wooded lake setting in the Wicklow Mountains south of present-day Dublin, offered a nevertheless harsh, remote abode. It is said that Kevin (or, in the Gaelic, *Coemgen*), a hermit who lived there in the sixth century, occupied "a hole in the rock wall of a cliff, emerging in winter to stand for hours stark naked in the icy waters of the lough [lake] or in summer to hurl himself—again naked—into a bush of poisonous nettles."[2] Interestingly, John O'Donovan, writer of *Wicklow Letters* (442 C.E.), refers to the place

where Kevin lived as the *Disert Coemgen*, that is, the "Desert of Coemgen´." As Losack and Rodgers note, "Kevin was at heart a hermit standing firmly in the orthodox desert spiritual tradition."[3]

Obviously, while these Celtic Christian sites were not located in desert regions, there was considerable desolation and deprivation. Giving up a relatively comfortable life to live at these harsh rocky or wooded monastic settings epitomized the denial of self in the face of God. Thus Kevin, Columba, and the other Celtic Christian monks who inhabited these remote Celtic wilderness retreats became known as "the green martyrs." This is as compared with "the red martyrs" who gave their lives for their faith, and "the white martyrs" who journeyed forth into missionary work that took them far and long from home.

It is perhaps ironic that Iona and Glendalough were eventually forced by the numbers of persons attracted to them to become larger monastic communities, places where great Christian scholarship and manuscript copying and illumination flourished. These communities became the precursors of the great medieval universities of Europe. People made pilgrimages to worship and study in these green monastic communities because they knew that in these remote wilderness places the early Christian Celts were in community with the One known as "I AM WHO I AM" (Exod. 3:14). This, of course, echoes a familiar teaching from one of the desert fathers:

"Go sit in your cell and your cell will teach you everything."

All this makes spiritual sense to me. Most of my life I have lived in climates where precipitation was frequent, in all its various forms, and the trees were leafy and green. For three and a half years, however, I lived in the high desert of southern Idaho near the Nevada border. There I came to understand how thirsty the Hebrew children were in the desert and why Jesus often alluded to the experience of thirst in his conversations and teaching.

I was surprised by the constant thirst I experienced in this climate where the average annual rainfall was only thirteen inches. During the summer the heat reminded me to drink water constantly. In fact, both my administrative assistant and I kept filled water tumblers at our desks at all times, simply drinking our way through the workday.

Winter was a different story. The cooler temperatures made me careless, daring me to think that since it was colder, I would not be so thirsty. How wrong I was! During the winter when I forgot to drink regularly I always found myself struck late in the afternoon by an incredible thirst that only a long evening of constant beverages could quench.

Other things were different in the desert, too. I could usually see for thirty to fifty miles atop a bluff because there was no foliage to block my vision, other than the occasional sagebrush. My eyesight, never very good, somehow adjusted to this, allowing me to see things at a long distance with great clarity. This was a development that startled me when I occasionally visited in the eastern United States during the summer. There I discovered that suddenly I could see not just a tree, but every single leaf and every crag in its bark simultaneously. My mother, an artist, explained this saying that in the desert I had developed what she called "artist eyes." All I knew was that I was seeing things as I had never seen them before.

Sandstorms, dust devils, and range fires also became part of my life. And lightning—oh, the lightning, furiously cracking straight up and down!—triggered my newfound artist's eyes to see every single thing illuminated in an instant. Often rain followed the lightning, but not much. So little rain fell that the usual result was simply a lingering smell of hot, damp dirt and sagebrush. In time I came to accept the reality that a "three-inch rain" in the arid American West meant that a few rain-drops fell three inches apart. Still, I found myself yearning for long, rainy days such as I had known in other places, and the wonderful smell that lingers after such rains.

Life for me was foreign in the desert, the wilderness. And yet in the midst of this dryness there was the pillar of light and cloud we call God. My faith and trust in God grew in the desert. At times, driving long distances in the desert alone, I was overcome by a sense of being totally exposed, with no protection from anything. I called that experience "exposophobia," that is, the opposite of acute, sickening claustrophobia. God came powerfully to me in those moments, offering the solace of divine companionship and a sense of protection. Likewise, during long, hot droughts my soul ached with homesickness for the revitalizing rains of more familiar places. Then suddenly, I would experience God as streams flowing in the desert. I thirsted and the water I received supplied all my needs. It made no intellectual sense, but my soul obtained all the sustenance it needed in that desolate wilderness.

My sojourn in the desert helped me to reclaim the stories I had learned in Sunday school as a child. These biblical accounts were interesting at the time, but they were also stories I could not personally attest to while growing up in a climate where rainstorms and deep snows fell in abundance. Living in the desert I remembered that in the wilderness Moses encountered the God who gave him the spiritual courage to lead the Hebrew children out of bondage. Their journey to freedom took them through the wilderness, where they and their descendants painfully came to trust God. In time, seasoned by their desert experience, they fought courageous battles in their quest for the land that would become home for them. Later, those same Hebrew children would experience a wilderness exile from that home. The exile proved to them once again that God, who was angry with them, would nevertheless go with them and remain with them.

God took Ezekiel to a dry, desolate valley and caused him to prophesy to the bones of battle-slaughtered warriors that hope and life are always breaking into our lives, even in the midst of death. John the Baptist went to the wilderness to preach a message proclaiming a baptism of repentance for the forgiveness of sins. Jesus was able to resist the temptations of greed, power, and blasphemy in the wilderness. Later he would use two fish and five loaves to feed thousands at the edge of the wilderness.

Over and over in the biblical record we read of times when the people of God experienced God's powerful presence while suffering in the wilderness. The Celtic Christians embraced this theme as their own. As Losack and Rodgers insightfully observe, "Eastern theology and pre-Christian Celtic religion combined to give Celtic Christianity a strongly creation-filled, as well as cross-centred, spirituality."[4] This, I believe, is the genius of the Celtic Christian desert experience: in the midst of celebrating the Creator we encounter the One whose agonizing death and life-giving resurrection saves creation. Thus there is an encounter with both a holiness and wholeness, a recovery of spiritual health focused on giving one's self over to the unknowns of the desert. Christians who surrender to the experience of God in the wilderness, whether it be in an inner-city neighborhood, forest, desert, deep wood, or prairie, find the strength, compassion, and courage to minister to others with hope and love.

Yes, there is suffering in our present-day wilderness. The number of impoverished people continues to soar in both inner-city as well as rural areas. Families abandoned by their fathers or mothers and the subsequent unraveling of community are cause for concern. Environmental misuse presents dangers for food production and water consumption. Violence, found in schools, on city streets, and in country homes, threatens the lives of those we love. The sin of racism continues to be rampant everywhere, fanned by the angry heat of paramilitary groups and other haters of human dignity. The lack of public transportation creates difficulties for those in need of medical care and supportive community. These problems, and a host of others, will not go away easily.

But as the early Celtic Christians came to know so well, God is always in the wilderness. This reality defies human logic while often bringing divine solutions. At the edge of the wilderness, food is miraculously multiplied. In the midst of loneliness, community emerges. Coalitions of like-minded persons are able to demand the restoration of strip-mined meadows and hills. Still others demand the removal of various kinds of pollution that poison water tables. Dedicated peacemakers say "No!" to the twin sins of racism and related violence. Wounded spirits who have known the deprivations of desert life bind together, generously providing transportation, education and training, and job incentives. These persons have learned to trust the promise of Isaiah:

> The wilderness and the dry land shall be glad,
>   the desert shall rejoice and blossom;
> like the crocus it shall blossom abundantly,
>   and rejoice with joy and singing.
> The glory of Lebanon shall be given to it,
>   the majesty of Carmel and Sharon.
> They shall see the glory of the LORD,
>   the majesty of our God.
>
> (Isaiah 35:1–2)

It makes no sense that the desert shall burst forth into beauty. But those who embrace this promise, those who fold the wings of the intellect and open the doors of their hearts, will find spiritual refreshment in desolate places. That is what makes the desert, the wilderness, holy ground.

$\mathcal{T}$HE ENCIRCLING PRESENCE

Stand in a place that is holy ground to you. Extend your hand before you and point your index finger forward. As if on a pivot, turn, using your finger to draw a circle around yourself. You have just performed the *Caim*, "the Encircling." The *Caim* is a Celtic Christian acknowledgment of the presence of God, reminding us of the protection from danger and evil that God offers to each of us. It is not performing the *Caim* itself that provides shelter—God's presence is already with us. The *Caim* simply reminds us of this holy reality. The following prayer, written in the early twentieth century, reflects the Celtic Christian understanding of the *Caim*.

> Circle me O God
> Keep hope within
> Despair without.
>
> Circle me O God
> Keep peace within
> Keep turmoil out.

Circle me O God
Keep calm within
Keep storms without.

Circle me O God
Keep strength within
Keep weakness out.[1]

There are times in our lives, such as when we experience sickness, fear, grief, or disappointment, when it is both good and necessary to pray the *Caim*. There is a profound sense of the divine in this supplication. The Celtic Christians offered many such petitions and called them protection prayers. We have already encountered part of St. Patrick's Breastplate Prayer in chapter 5. Three additional lines from this prayer reflect the *Caim*:

Christ with me, Christ before me, Christ behind me,
Christ within me, Christ beneath me, Christ above me.
Christ on my right, Christ on my left.

The sentiment expressed in this prayer is similar to the thought of Paul, who listed all the general categories of things in this life that can threaten our well-being: trouble, hardship, persecution, famine, nakedness, danger, and the threat of violence. Then Paul emphatically states that nothing can separate us from the love of Christ (Rom. 8:35–39). Likewise, St. Patrick's Breastplate Prayer echoes a parallel theme: if we envision ourselves as surrounded by the presence of the risen and victorious Christ, nothing can hurt us.

I have always loved the Greek word *en*, the word for *in* as it is generally found in the New Testament. The actual meaning of the word in Greek is not "in" but rather "within." That is, we believe within the love of Christ. We trust within the protection of Christ. We do not submit to despair because we dwell within the healing touch of Christ. This is what it means to trust and live the Caim.

The circle was an ever-present symbol for the pagan Celts. The Celts were unable to decorate things simply, so they usually overdid it in circular-patterned, joyful, childish glee. The circle often appeared in spirals, probably representing the pattern formed in water after a stone is thrown into a pool or well, another symbol important to the Celts. For them these holy waters symbolized both life and deep connections to the earth. The following must have been heady words falling on the ears of the Celts with their affection for what they called sacred wells:

Jesus said to her [the Samaritan woman at the well],
"Everyone who drinks of this water will be thirsty
again, but those who drink of the water that I will
give them will never be thirsty. The water that I will
give will become in them a spring of water gushing
up to eternal life."

(John 4:13–14)

Given their fascination with circles and spirals, it is
not surprising that the Celtic Christians were quick to
superimpose the circle onto the cross. The ringed cross,
many of which were carved in the ninth and tenth
centuries, became the Celtic Christian synthesis of these
two powerful symbols. My own understanding of Celtic
Christianity grew and my artist's eye came to appreciate
the beautiful carved ringed crosses that I saw at the
churchyard cemetery at Monasterboice, a former monastic
settlement north of Dublin. These ornate crosses also
included intricately carved scenes from the Bible, biblical
stories in capsule form.

In time my pilgrimage from island to island and
from inspiration to inspiration seemed to me a circle,
always moving on to a new Celtic Christian thought only
to circle back to another and then begin again. In a sense
the circle became symbolic of my foray into Celtic
Christian spirituality. Like the islands I mentioned in the
Preface, irregular circles that they are, my faith journey
became and continues to be one of circles, each
accompanied by the encircling presence of God.

It is a matter of perception. One day at Tara I discovered that I could see the full 360-degree view only by turning in place and, degree by degree, gaining the full circular panorama. It reminded me of the Shaker song I have always loved, "Simple Gifts," with its spiraling refrain:

> When true simplicity is gained,
> To bow and to bend we shan't be ashamed.
> To turn, turn will be our delight,
> 'Till by turning, turning we come 'round right!

This refrain holds the same sentiment contained in words I found on a brochure which for several years sat propped on the bookshelves in my office. I don't remember what the brochure advertised, but the front of it said this:

> We shall not cease from exploration
> And the end of all our exploring
> Will be to arrive where we started
> And know the place for the first time.[2]

It may be that I quickly embraced the concept of the encircling presence of God because this refrain and this quotation were so patterned on my mind and heart. Or it may be that my encounter with Celtic Christianity simply enabled me to understand why the refrain and quotation had always been so important to me. I dwell in the circle of God's love. Within that circle my faith, hope, and love are secure.

Another aspect of encountering Celtic Christianity that I did not anticipate was a confrontation with my own theology—my understanding of God and how God has chosen to relate to human beings. To be frank, I thought I had put the days of seminary theology courses long behind me. To me theology had become a practical tool, a way to think about congregations and help them grow in numbers and ministry. When I thought about grace, even the saving grace that empowers and sustains my faith and ministry, I was too quick to leap from the personal experience of grace to how to use the message of grace to further the vitality of congregations. Some might call that a misuse, even a prostitution, of theology. And then, as I journeyed into Celtic Christianity, I met Pelagius. The great saints of Celtic Christianity are Brigid, Columba, and Patrick. Pelagius is the great theologian of Celtic Christianity, one whose thinking is at once both insightful and disturbing. Some (including many church historians) might say he is the great heretic of Celtic Christianity, but I think that is too strong a statement. I am grateful to him. Following and tracking the thinking of Pelagius brought me full circle back to wrestling once again with who the Christ is for me and those I seek to serve.

A rather significant controversy broke out between the Celtic Christians and the Roman Christians during the early years of this period that focused on the conflicting theologies of Augustine of Hippo and

Pelagius. Augustine had frolicked in an extremely licentious early adult period in which he fully embraced the epicurean doctrine of wine, women, and song (and lots of each!). Eventually, he experienced a reconversion to the Christianity of his parents, dismissed his faithful mistress, and proceeded to write his epic *Confessions*. In this work, which records his own prodigal return to Christianity amidst what appears to be a nervous breakdown, Augustine asserted that we are born evil because of Adam and Eve's fall from grace. He called this the doctrine of original sin. Augustine asserted that without the unmerited grace of God there is no hope for humanity.

It is true, of course, that we are saved by grace. Augustine's work, however, was disturbing to some at that time and remains so today. We must remember that on his journey to his theological conclusions Augustine enjoyed a considerable variety of worldly and carnal pleasures. And then suddenly, Augustine's antidote for humanity, in addition to accepting God's grace, was that humans should live dull and generally not pleasurable lives. He no longer saw anything in the human reality of creation as containing any goodness. Many Christian theologians perceive that Augustine came to believe that women, in particular, were inherently evil. Evidently Augustine never read Genesis 1:31: "God saw everything that he had made, and indeed, it was very good."

Meanwhile, a Celt named Pelagius, most likely from Britain, developed an alternative approach to Christian doctrine in which he suggested that humanity did not need divine grace. He asserted that while Adam and Eve had provided a bad example of humans relating to God, Jesus of Nazareth provided the perfect example. Thus, all one had to do was engage in this *impeccantia*, this "possibility of living without sin." Easier said than done, of course. The dilemma over Augustine and Pelagius's thoughts lingers still today, with one part of the Christian community wanting to embrace Augustine's concept of grace, and the other wanting to celebrate and preserve that which is good in this world.

Pelagius was summoned before various popes and bishops and even visited Augustine upon one occasion to argue his mistaken doctrine. Eventually he was condemned and excommunicated, but he disappeared mysteriously on his way home to Britain. Some think he may have assumed a different identity and became a priest.

Despite Pelagius's condemnation and excommunication, the die was cast. Most Celtic Christians embraced his teachings, and the Pelagian impact lingered for centuries. Patrick himself reflects Pelagius's teachings in some aspects. While he did teach the Irish Celts the basic gospel story, he did not try to change their joy of human and earthly life. Perhaps he recognized in their joy a celebration of God's created world as good, while still maintaining the need for the death of Christ to atone for human sin and the resurrection as a sign of Christ's victory over sin and death.

I believe Augustine was theologically correct in his understanding of grace. As both the apostle Paul and Martin Luther asserted, we are saved by grace. My sympathies, however, also lie with the Irish Celtic Christians who rejected Augustine because he condemned almost everything their Celtic culture revered: creation itself, including a celebration of human sexuality and human enjoyment of God's handiwork.

Reflecting upon the teachings of Augustine of Hippo and Pelagius sometimes caused me to feel as if I was spinning in theological circles. In the midst of reflecting upon the differences between them I was forced to ask myself which doctrine drives my own sense of Christian spirituality. The answer was both. I do not want to live in this world, with all its temptations and dangers, without the possibility of being saved by the grace of God. However, I do not want to live in this world if I cannot enjoy the good things that God has created for all of humanity. By *enjoy* I do not mean wanton debauchery rife with irresponsible uses of creation. Rather I want to enjoy creation with an awareness of what respectful Christian stewardship means coupled with an awareness of that behavior which most allows me to glorify God. This, I believe, is full participation in God's creation, full celebration, and full enjoyment.

Therefore this is what I celebrate about Pelagius's teaching: that it allows me to reach out with joy and love to embrace the fullness of creation. I do not have to be ashamed of the beauty I enjoy. Unlike Augustine, I do not believe that I need to be saved from this enjoyment. In fact, I believe that I was saved by the grace of God for it. The Word of God, as contained in scripture, demands that we respond to the grace of God if the salvation we receive is to be fully effective. To respond with gratitude for the gift of creation and engage in meaningful celebration of it is a valid expression of the Christian faith, one heartily affirmed in Celtic Christian spirituality.

I have come to understand that Celtic Christianity embraces the totality of life and living while acknowledging what God has done for us in Jesus the Christ. This is what makes Celtic Christianity remarkably holistic and healthy. As Anthony Duncan comments:

> Celtic Christianity takes the total person in its stride and denies nothing, shies away from nothing, consecrates everything. It also "remembers its manners" and keeps a respectful distance from those things that are not its concern—but without denying them.[3]

Duncan's words are really not radical. In fact, we sing this sentiment frequently from our hymnbooks.

Hymns like "For the Beauty of the Earth," quoted at the beginning of this book, and others such as "Fairest Lord Jesus," "Morning Has Broken," and "All Things Bright and Beautiful" sweetly echo Celtic Christian spirituality each time we sing them. If we truly pay attention to the lyrics when we sing these hymns, we will faithfully acknowledge that

> the Celtic Christian tradition can, if we will allow it to do so, rescue us from a vision grown too narrow, a God, interpreted in our own image, who is far too small and a cramped, bickering ecclesiasticism masquerading as the entire Kingdom of God. It can set our feet back firmly in the Way.[4]

But the Way, from the Celtic Christian point of view, is circular, not linear. We journey in spiraling circles of faith and experience, and we dwell within that circle of love that is God. We have our being within God. For those whose lives are dominated by events and timelines, this may be hard to comprehend. But those of us who embrace the encircling presence of God cannot comprehend life with the Divinity in any other manner.

Not long ago I spent the better part of an afternoon dozing on the sofa during a lingering thunderstorm. Anxious to resume working at my computer, but reluctant to turn it on in the midst of the storm, I occasionally tuned into the Weather Channel on television. Every ten minutes the broadcast showed the local weather map, and it confirmed what I suspected. We were in the midst of one of those summer thunderstorms that meander into western New York from Lake Erie and then appear to get stuck in the foothills of the Allegheny Mountains. The storm, large and circular in shape, simply enveloped our area, bathing us in warm summer rain while constantly reminding us of its presence with lightning followed by the gentle rumble of thunder.

The storm was simply a presence throughout the afternoon. I have known and experienced similar storms since childhood. They have always reminded me of the presence of God: refreshingly close, encircling me, and rumbling with the holy reminder of the Voice of the Ages. This is the storm that echoes the words:

> The voice of the LORD is over the waters;
>> the God of glory thunders,
>> the LORD, over mighty waters.
> The voice of the LORD is powerful;
>> the voice of the LORD is full of majesty.
>>> (Psalm 29:3–4)

What does it mean to live as Patrick did, believing that we are safe and protected because we dwell within the presence of God? To answer that question we would have to put ourselves into Patrick's shoes and experience the horror of being kidnapped, forced into slavery, and exposed to fearsome weather and beasts. Can't imagine all

that? Then imagine what you fear most. I know what it feels like to be flying into Chicago's O'Hare International airport, the plane approaching the runway for landing, and then suddenly have the plane lurch back into the air at an extremely sharp angle. I knew instantly that the pilot had recognized that we were in danger of a midair collision and I remember exactly how I felt at that moment: sheer terror. A sickening silence prevailed until the pilot finally leveled off the plane and then announced to us that we had, indeed, barely avoided colliding with another airplane. I do not dwell on that memory, but so terrifying is it that I can readily recall it.

Another fearsome moment that comes to mind is a day in the Bighorn Mountains in Wyoming. I was walking through brush toward a scenic viewpoint on a canyon rim when suddenly I heard the loud, unmistakable warning of a rattlesnake. My blood ran cold as I abruptly stopped, cautiously looking around myself. But I could not see the feared serpent, I could only hear it. My heart seemed to stop beating, I could not breathe, and the hairs on the back of my neck quite literally stood on end. I was

utterly terrified. Only when I realized that the snake was
on a ledge below the canyon rim did I finally relax and
make my way from that place.

You may know terror in your own life, such as
what it feels like to be the victim of violence or to receive
a diagnosis of cancer. If we are to live with Christian faith
in these moments, however, even as Patrick did, if we are
to believe we are safe and protected, then we must trust
the all-encompassing promise of Christ with us, before us,
above us, below us, and behind us. Encircled by Christ,
we can be confident in the power of God. When despair
descends upon us we can trust God to see us safely
through the night terror of our souls.

Yes, we often feel challenged, saddened, and
afraid. But God is with us, encircling us. God cannot
make hard times go away easily, but God surrounds and
upholds us in those times. Breathing the *Caim* in our
souls, we can stand secure and at peace on holy ground.

EPILOGUE

I began this pilgrimage because I was searching for a new Christian spiritual expression in my own life. In addition, something deep inside me, perhaps curiosity, although it felt stronger than that, drove me to explore what insights dwelled in the meager spiritual inheritance my father bequeathed to me. Because of his Irish roots, I thought I might find clues to his spirituality in Ireland. I wondered if it descended from his own Irish parents and grandparents, perhaps reaching back for several generations. Embarking on the study, research, and meditation at the beginning of my journey, I did not know that I was about to launch into an in-depth encounter with Celtic Christian spirituality. I more or less stumbled into it.

Stumbling is a good word to describe this journey, for I left Ireland with still-fuzzy impressions of my father's spirituality. That fuzziness lingers today despite other journeys and continued encounters with Celtic Christian spirituality. Maybe that is the way it is meant to be. As Leon Uris writes in his novel *Redemption*, which tells of Irish life from the late 1800s through the early 1900s, "We all seem to spend the second half of our lives getting over the first half." Usually the first half is the part of our lives in which our parents played a significant role.

I returned from my pilgrimage still longing to know more about my father's enigmatic faith but resigned to the fact that that may not be possible in this life. Still, I am grateful that despite its shortcomings, his faith set me on a pilgrimage. Like Patrick, whom Oisín called from his prayers, I was called away from my ecclesiastical busyness to this journey. My pilgrimage took me deep into the woods. There I found out more about myself and more about God.

One Irish legend says that there is a pot of gold at the end of the rainbow and that if you can catch a leprechaun and hold onto him, he will take you to the riches. Although I was told they are very common due to the wet and changeable climate, I saw only one rainbow during my pilgrimage to Ireland. Much to my surprise, where it touched the earth there was a surreal golden glow!

I went to Ireland searching for a spiritual inheritance that I thought was hidden in my father's past. But, like the elusive leprechaun's gold and that golden glow I found at the end of the rainbow, I could not grasp my father's spirituality. What I did obtain, however, was a powerful reminder that God granted me (and you, too) the greatest spiritual legacy of all: faith in Jesus the Christ. It was those "foolish Galatians" who helped me to relearn this biblical truth.

Throughout my Celtic Christian pilgrimage I have continued to be astonished that the Galatians, located in Asia Minor, were themselves Celtic cousins of the Celts of Brittany and the British Isles. I might never have paid attention to them except for my pilgrimage through Celtic Christian spirituality.

The apostle Paul wrote to the first-century Christian Celts in Galatia because after his departure they had begun to cling to the law of the Hebrew scriptures, rather than to faith in the Christ and him crucified and risen. Paul reminded them of "then," before faith came, and "now," the present reality, itself the result of the Christ's death on the cross and his subsequent resurrection. Once again, Paul's words:

> You foolish Galatians! Who has bewitched you? It was before your eyes that Jesus Christ was publicly exhibited as crucified! The only thing I want to learn from you is this: Did you receive the Spirit by doing the works of the law or by believing what you heard? Are you so foolish? Having started with the Spirit, are you now ending with the flesh?
>
> (Galatians 3:1–3)

Paul further explained to the Galatians that they had become children of God through faith in Jesus Christ. He said they were part of God's *tuath*, God's clan or tribe. He also reminded them that through Abraham

God's promises were made to all of Abraham's descendants, including the Gentiles, of which the Celts in Galatia were a part: "Now the promises were made to Abraham and to his offspring. . . . For if the inheritance comes from the law, it no longer comes from the promise; but God granted it to Abraham through the promise" (Gal. 3:16, 18).

Just in case the Galatians still did not understand, Paul concluded his treatise with these words:

> In Christ Jesus you are all children of God through faith. As many of you as were baptized into Christ have clothed yourselves with Christ. There is no longer Jew or Greek, there is no longer slave or free, there is no longer male and female; for all of you are one in Christ Jesus. And if you belong to Christ, then you are Abraham's offspring, heirs according to the promise.
>
> (Galatians 3:26–29)

How could a Celt not love these words? The Celt in me loves them. In them I found the inheritance I was seeking—an adoption, a fosterage of God's own choosing! And with this insight, this vision, I realized that I had come full circle to the Christian faith that has been the cornerstone of my life.

Again, in Uris's words, "We all seem to spend the second half of our lives getting over the first half." Early on I read a preliminary draft of this book to a rural ministry class I was teaching, and then I let close friends read it. In feedback my readers told me recollections of deer hunting with their dads, stories about their Celtic ancestors coming to America, and encounters they had experienced with plants and animals. Few of these folks, however, were able to share connections between their stories and their experience of God as Creator. I realized that my writing was not setting their minds and hearts free. Rather the images were miring them in the past, in their family histories and relationships. I was troubled because they did not understand that Celtic Christianity is far more than a mere sentimental spirituality. Rather, it points us to God as described in the Preface: Creator, Redeemer, and Holy Wind dancing in the sunlight on the beach and pounding in the crest of the waves. In time I realized that even as I had to let go of my father's elusive spiritual legacy, I needed to gently encourage others to let go of their pasts and engage Celtic Christianity as a journey into their own spiritual future.

In recent years, family systems theory, as taught by Murray Bowen, has helped us see that very often what we are, how we think, and what we become is heavily influenced by our interaction with our parents, grandparents, and the ghostly legacies of our families' histories, ethnic backgrounds, stories, and traditions.[1] This is true. But it is not enough. Only God is truly enough. Only the legacy we receive from God provides the ultimate inheritance our souls crave. This bequest helps us break loose from the first part of our lives and journey on to the rest.

I have repeated the image of standing on holy ground throughout these pages. Perhaps in closing it would be better to say that by the grace of God we are journeying on good and holy ground. We know where we have been, we know whose we are, and we feel God's vision forming in our hearts. Having experienced the rich Celtic Christian perspective we have new understanding of the divine mysteries that link sound and sight, heart and mind. This is not a new faith I have shared with you. It is a renewing and reviving way of envisioning the Christian faith with powerful images—holy earth, leaping deer, wild geese, darkness and light, fire with all its majesty, the howling, comforting wilderness—that can illuminate the sacred wells of your own life. It is vision surrounded by the Way, the Truth, and the Life (see John 14:6 *a*). It is a visionary journey taken on holy ground.

As I write these words, it is early summer. The woods all around me are full of a dazzling celebration of the color green: the emerald richness of maple leaves; the deep green of pine trees; the olives, lime-greens, and yellow-greens of the grass and brush. Overhead a dense canopy of tree branches keeps me dry even during a gentle rain. The stream with its lilting music wanders by our deck. With some imagination I can picture myself at a early Celtic Christian monastery like Glendalough.

But my experience is not one of deprivation and I cannot count myself a green martyr like Kevin and his fellow monks. Rather my experience is one of a rich, deep inheritance of faith, with an assurance I did not have before I began my journey with Celtic Christian spirituality. I am now confident that I may love both Christ and God's creation with all my heart, mind, and soul.

In my lap lies dozing a new puppy who has come to make his home with us. He is warm and friendly and has already returned laughter to our hearts. His presence reminds us that God the Creator is good and provides for all our needs. Our souls are restored. The leap of the deer rustles in the nearby woods.

> For the joy of ear and eye,
> for the heart and mind's delight,
> for the mystic harmony
> linking sense to sound and sight,
>
> Lord of all,
> to thee we raise
> this our hymn of grateful praise.

ANNOTATED BIBLIOGRAPHY

Benwick, James. *Irish Druids and Old Irish Religions*. Dorset: Dorset Press, 1986.
A classic work which examines Irish druids, old Irish religions, and the integration of Christianity into these Celtic streams.

Bradley, Ian. *Columba: Pilgrim and Penitent*. Glasgow: Wild Goose Publications, 1996.
This readable book addresses the key themes of Saint Columba's life: pilgrimage, penitence, and politics. The reader will enjoy this scholarly, yet simple, portrait of Iona's founder.

Cahill, Thomas. *How the Irish Saved Civilization*. New York: Doubleday, 1995.
This New York Times Bestseller helps the reader understand how Ireland enjoyed a "Golden Age" while Europe languished in the Dark Ages. A playful, bold, lively retelling of the Celtic Christian experience.

De Paor, Liam. *Saint Patrick's World*. Notre Dame, Ind.: University of Notre Dame Press, 1993.
An important addition to academic Celtic Christian literature, this book examines two writings of Patrick himself, plus other original texts from Patrick's era. Serious students of Patrick will appreciate the book's depth as well as its examination of related medieval writings.

Duncan, Anthony. *The Elements of Celtic Christianity*. Rockport, Mass.: Element Books, 1992.
An excellent overview of Celtic Christianity that links this distinctive spirituality to the ecological issues of this present age.

Ellis, Peter Berresford. *Celtic Inheritance*. London: Constable, 1992.
A comprehensive study of Celtic Christianity which presents a general history of the subject, organized into geographical Celtic regions. Annotated pen and ink drawings provide helpful illustrations throughout the book.

Galloway, Kathy, ed. *The Pattern of Our Days: Liturgies and*

Resources for Worship. Glasgow: Wild Goose Publications, 1996.
These liturgies and other worship resources have emerged from the present-day Iona Community. This creative collection includes liturgies of pilgrimage, healing, and light as well as prayers for forgiveness, thanksgiving, and blessing.

Mackey, James P., ed. *An Introduction to Celtic Christianity*. Edinburgh: T & T Clark Ltd., 1995.
Fourteen essays for the serious Celtic Christian reader which explore the Celtic consciousness and resultant expressions of this spirituality. The book is mysterious, remarkable, and splendid.

O'Driscoll, Herbert. *The Leap of the Deer*. Boston: Cowley Publications, 1994.
O'Driscoll's memories of a Celtic childhood form the background for this exploration of Celtic Christian spirituality. This excellent storyteller retells his journey from rural Ireland to the priesthood with grace and hope.

O Riordáin, John J. *The Music of What Happens*. Dublin: The Columba Press, 1996.
Focusing on the communal nature of Celtism, the author relates the ancient themes of Celtic spirituality to modern Ireland. By joining together the community of saints and the fullness of the Trinity in his writing, O Riordáin celebrates the "sweet music" of the Celtic Christian experience.

Powell, T. G. E. *The Celts*. London: Thames and Hudson, 1958.
A seminal text about the Celts. This book provides an overview of Celtic history, archeology, and linguistics as found throughout Europe. A large number of illustrations add to the book's richness.

Rodgers, Michael, and Marcus Losack. *Glendalough: A Celtic Pilgrimage*. Harrisburg, Pa.: Morehouse Publishing, 1996.
The authors present a pictorial and literary journey to this ancient Celtic Christian "monastic city." This book will delight those who have visited or hope to visit Glendalough, hermitage of Saint Kevin.

Simms, George Otto. *St. Patrick: The Real Story of Patrick*. Dublin: The O'Brien Press, 1991.
Although written for the youth reader, this book tells the authentic story of Patrick in a simple yet detailed manner.

NOTES

Chapter 1: All the Earth Is Sacred
1. Michael Rodgers and Marcus Losack, *Glendalough: A Celtic Pilgrimage* (Harrisburg, Pa.: Morehouse Publishing, 1996), 39.
2. A. Carmichael, *Carmina Gadelica*, Vol. I (Scottish Academic Press, 1928), 271, as quoted in Anthony Duncan, *The Elements of Celtic Christianity* (Rockport, Mass.: Element Books, Inc., 1992), 105.

Chapter 2: Holy Boy, Holy Journey
1. Caitlan Matthews, *Celtic Devotional* (Dublin: Godsfield Press United, 1996), 10.
2. F. Delaney, *The Celts* (Grafton, 1989), as quoted in Duncan, *The Elements of Celtic Christianity*, 6.
3. Robert Welch, ed., *W. B. Yeats: Writings on Irish Folklore, Legend and Myth* (New York: Penguin Books, 1993), xxv.

Chapter 3: Leaping Deer and Wild Geese
1. Rodgers and Losak, *Glendalough: A Celtic Pilgrimage*, 103.

Chapter 4: Turning Darkness into Light
1. Thomas Cahill, *How the Irish Saved Civilization* (New York: Doubleday, 1995), 162–163, except the last stanza: source unknown.

Chapter 5: Smooring the Fire
1. Thomas Cahill, *How the Irish Saved Civilization*, 116–117.
2. Andy Raine and John T. Skinner, comp., *Celtic Daily Prayer* (London: HarperCollins Religious, 1994), 138.
3. Rodgers and Losack, *Glendalough: A Celtic Pilgrimage*, 36.
4. Lesley Whiteside, *The Spirituality of St. Patrick* (Harrisburg, Pa.: Morehouse Publishing, 1997), 45.
5. Esther de Waal, *The Celtic Vision* (Petersham, Mass.: St. Bede's Publications, 1988), 77.

Chapter 6: In the Howling, Comforting Wilderness
1. Welch, ed., *W. B. Yeats: Writings on Irish Folklore, Legend and Myth*, xix.

2. Cahill, *How the Irish Saved Civilization*, 156.
3. Rodgers and Losack, *Glendalough: A Celtic Pilgrimage*, 110.
4. Ibid., 93.

Chapter 7: The Encircling Presence

1. Kuno Meyer, *Selections from Ancient Irish Poetry*, as quoted in David Adam, *The Cry of the Deer* (Harrisburg, Pa.: Morehouse Publishing, 1987), 12, 13.
2. T. S. Eliot, "Little Gidding," in *Four Quartets* (New York: Harcourt, Brace & World, 1943), 39.
3. Duncan, *The Elements of Celtic Christianity*, 108.
4. Ibid., 112.

Epilogue

1. Murray Bowen and Michael E. Kerr, *Family Evaluation: An Approach Based on Bowen Theory* (New York: W. W. Norton & Co., 1988).